Point
Well Taken

The Guide to Success with Needles & Threads

An In Cahoots® book
by Debbie Garbers and Janet F. O'Brien

Point Well Taken
The Guide to Success with Needles & Threads
Copyright © 1996 In Cahoots®
ISBN 0-9653079-0-5

Revision 2

All rights reserved
Published in Roswell, Georgia
In Cahoots
P O Box 72336
Marietta, GA 30007-2336 USA
770-641-0945

We have worked hard to make this book accurate, complete, and easy to follow. However, In Cahoots cannot guarantee results since selection of supplies and procedures vary. No warranty is implied, and In Cahoots assumes no responsibility for use of this information.

Product descriptions in this book are from the best available information in the spring of 1996. Of course, manufacturers constantly expand and change their product lines, so check with your dealer for availability.

Fibers and other products vary widely in availability and quality. Whenever specific brand names are mentioned, it usually means the authors have used the products and were pleased with the results. If you're having trouble using a product that is not listed in this resource guide, try one of the products listed in this guide to make sure the problem is not with your machine or sewing technique.

The use of brand names in this guide is also intended to save readers time. There may be other products that are comparable. Be sure to test with the exact project materials, especially when working with unfamiliar fabrics and threads.

Printed in the United States of America

About the Authors

Debbie Garbers and Janet O'Brien are garment designers and teachers with a special interest in embellishment, textures, fibers, and colors. They believe art-to-wear clothing should enhance the wearer and satisfy the creative sewer. Their philosophy carries over to their teaching and writing. They develop classes and patterns so the average sewer can enjoy creating her own artful garments and accessories.

Debbie and Janet met about five years ago in a surface design class. They both had learned sewing and needlecrafts as children and were looking for new ways to use their sewing machines. They kept bumping into each other in classes and meetings where they shared information and their sewing enthusiasm.

Not only do Debbie and Janet share a love of sewing, but they also have similar education backgrounds. Debbie has a Master's Degree in Special Education, and Janet has a Ph.D. in Elementary Education. Debbie taught kindergarten children with special needs while Janet taught adults and wrote technical references. In addition, they both have retail experience.

When Debbie and Janet began teaching together in 1993, they saw the need for flattering art-to-wear patterns with thorough directions. As a result, they started In Cahoots to fill this void. They now have six garment patterns that include embellishment, piecing, and pin weaving techniques. All of the patterns are classroom tested before production, and all include thorough instructions with clear drawings. The embellished vest patterns have helpful information about decorative threads as well as detailed machine set-up directions for each technique. These patterns are available at local quilt and sewing shops or directly from In Cahoots.

Nationally recognized for their garment designs, Debbie and Janet have a vest in the 1995 Sulky book, *Embellishing Concepts in Sulky*. Janet won a first place ribbon in the Sewing with Nancy Challenge. Debbie had a five-piece ensemble in the 1995 American Quilter's Society Fashion Show and vests in the '94 and '95 Hoffman Challenge clothing exhibit. Both Debbie and Janet had two ensembles in the 1996 Mid-Atlantic Wearable Art Festival. Janet has a three-piece ensemble in the 1996 American Quilter's Society Fashion Show. They are creating an ensemble for the 1996 Fairfield Fashion show.

Acknowledgments

After teaching consumers, shop owners, and shop teachers about needles and threads over the past four years, we have finally condensed our "teaching notes" into this book. It was the encouragement from our students that made us even consider such an undertaking.

We'd like to thank our mothers, grandmothers, and aunts, who helped us learn how to sew. We'd also like to thank the teachers who have shared their knowledge of sewing with us.

Of all the people who've helped us in this endeavor, we'd like to offer a special thanks to our illustrator, editor, and computer wizard, Jeff Garbers.

Without the support of our families, this book would have been impossible. Thank you — Jeff, Kathy, Ray, Betty, Jim, and Alison.

Trademarks and Brand Names Listed in This Book

We have made every attempt to properly credit the trademarks and brand names listed in this book.
We apologize for any that are not listed correctly.

Alcazar™ is a trademark of Pfaff Germany
Aqua-Solv™ is a trademark of Sew Art International
Big Foot is a brand name of Little Foot, Ltd.
Creative Feet™ is a trademark of Creative Feet
DMC® is a registered trademark of Dollfus-Mieg & Cie. SA
Dritz® is a registered trademark of John Dritz & Sons
Gütermann® is a registered trademark of Gütermann & Co.
In Cahoots® is a registered trademark of In Cahoots
J & P Coats® is a registered trademark of J & P Coats
Kanagawa is a brand name of YLI Corporation
Little Foot™ is a trademark of Little Foot, Ltd.
Madeira® is a registered trademark of Madeira Threads (UK) Ltd.
Metafil® is a registered trademark of Mbassociates
Metrosene is a brand name of Arova Mettler AG
Mettler is a brand name of Arova Mettler AG
Mez-Alcazar™ is a trademark of Pfaff Germany
Natesh® is a registered trademark of Kaleidoscope
Pearls & Piping™ is a trademark of Creative Feet
Perfect Sew® is a registered trademark of Palmer Pletsch Publishing
Post-It™ is a trademark of 3M
Press and Tear is a brand name of Sew Art International
Satin Edge™ is a trademark of Creative Feet
Schmetz is a brand name of Ferd. Schmetz GmbH, Germany
Sequins & Ribbon™ is a trademark of Creative Feet
Singer® is a registered trademark of Singer Manufacturing Co.
Solvy™ is a trademark of Sulky of America
Stitch and Tear® is a registered trademark of Fredenberg Nonwovens, Pellon® Division
Sulky® is a registered trademark of Gunold & Stickma
Tear-Away is a brand name of Sew Art International
Teflon® is a registered trademark of E.I. duPont de Nemours & Co.
That Patchwork Place® is a registered trademark of That Patchwork Place, Inc.
ThreadFuse™ is a trademark of the Perfect Notion Co.
Tire™ is a trademark of Fuji Sen-Ico
Totally Stable is a brand name of Sulky of America

Table of Contents

Introduction

Today's sewing offers us so many choices in the fabrics to select and the projects to undertake. However, we shouldn't take for granted the sewing products we use the most — our needles and threads. Spending time to select the best needle and thread for a project will make sewing easier, reduce frustration, and go a long way to making the project enjoyable and wonderful.

We wrote this book with many readers in mind:

- New sewers who face making many choices and decisions that can be overwhelming for even simple projects.

- Returning sewers who want to take advantage of all of the new products that make sewing easier and quicker and give better results.

- Sewers and quilters who have done basic sewing and now want to add a dash of embellishment to projects.

- Sewers and quilters who want to use innovative techniques and expand their creative repertoire.

- Sewers and quilters who help others make sewing decisions.

Everyone will learn something new by reading this book, and as a result, their sewing will improve. This resource gives you the information you need to help you begin your new project with confidence. The basic information is accompanied by helpful tips to make your sewing easier.

We encourage you to create your own challenges. Try to push yourself just a little bit further with each project. It's okay to leave some of those UFO's unfinished. Above all, don't be hard on yourself (say the two who are trying this philosophy themselves). Sewing is rewarding and relaxing; it's not without its moments of frustration and mistakes, but it's cheaper than a psychiatrist, and a *lot* more fun.

Use *Point Well Taken* as a reference, but also take time to play, experiment, and discover for yourself!

How to Use This Book

We recommend that you take a few minutes to look through this book, making note of particular items and tips of interest. Then pull it out as a reference for your sewing projects. For those who wish to take some time to explore stitching possibilities, we suggest using this book as an outline. Time spent experimenting will pay off in trying new needles and threads, fine-tuning old stitching methods, plus discovering many new fiber and stitch combinations. You will learn so much more about your machine and grow to love it even more.

If you would like to add your own samples of stitches and threads to this book, you can take it to a good copy place, have them remove the binding, punch three holes in the left margin, and put it into a three-ring binder. We suggest you place the samples in plastic page protectors rather than gluing them on to the paper. For more information about making your own "stitches notebook," see the tip under *Decorative Threads*, page 32.

Getting Started

There is rarely *one* right way to sew a particular project. The goal is to find the combination of fabric, needles, and threads that gives you the results you want. When making your selections, there are a few general rules to keep in mind.

- The best needle for a project is a new needle.

- First, choose the sewing thread to match the fabric. The *Basic Threads* and *Special Purpose Threads* chapters will help you make this decision.

- Next, choose the needle type to match the fabric. The *Basic Needles* and *Special Purpose Needles* chapters will help you make this decision.

- Finally, choose the needle size to match the fabric and thread. Match the needle size to the thread remembering that a fine thread in a larger needle may not form the stitches properly.

- A project may require several different types of needles for different purposes. For example, to construct a cotton knit shorts set, use a Stretch 80/12 needle with all-purpose polyester thread. To hem and topstitch the set, use a Stretch Twin 2.5 or 4.0 and all-purpose polyester or rayon decorative thread.

- For decorative sewing and embellishing, anything goes. You are only limited by your imagination. The *Decorative Needles* and *Decorative Threads* chapters will help you make these decisions.

⚷ *TIP: Use the* Needles & Threads Chart *on pages 54 - 55 as a quick reference when you select needles and threads. Heavy, densely woven fabrics may require a stronger needle than those recommended in the chart. Test stitch with the recommended needle first and check to be sure the machine is forming perfectly balanced stitches.*

⚷ *TIP: The* Decorative Needles & Threads Chart *on page 56 will help you match decorative threads and needles, and the* Twin Needles Chart *on page 57 pairs twin needle sizes with the appropriate presser foot for your sewing needs.*

IMPORTANT NOTE: Before changing machine settings, make a note of the settings you use for regular sewing. Also note the tension for both needle and bobbin if you plan to change either of these. This will save you a lot of time later!

What is a Machine Needle?

Webster's New World Dictionary defines *needle* as "a small, slender, sharp-pointed piece of steel with a hole for thread, used for sewing."

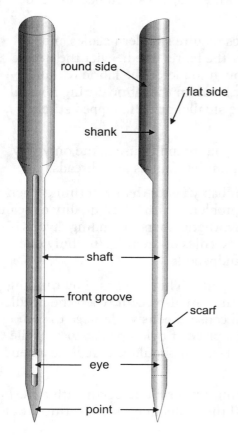

Point: One of the main differences between needles is the type of point. Points can be sharp, ball-point, knife blade, or universal, and needles are generally named for their type of point. You'll select a point type that works well with your fabric selection, which we'll discuss in detail later under *Basic Needles* and *Special Purpose Needles*.

Eye: The eye is the hole through which the thread passes. As the needle size increases, the size of the eye increases.

Shank: The shank is the part of the needle that is inserted into the machine. Today's machine needles have a shank with a flat back, so you won't insert them backwards. The shank size increases as the needle size increases.

Shaft: The shaft is the body of the needle. The needle size on the package is an indication of the relative thickness of the shaft.

Scarf: The scarf is the indentation at the back of the needle around the eye. A stitch is formed when the bobbin shuttle swings into the scarf, and hooks into the looped needle thread. The long scarf on the universal, sharp, and ball-point needles helps to eliminate skipped stitches.

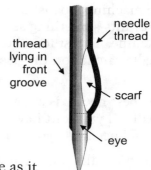

Front Groove: The front groove allows thread to remain close to the needle as it travels down the needle towards the bobbin. The deep groove of some needles helps to protect threads from friction created when piercing the fabric. If the needle is too fine for the size of the thread, there is not enough room for the thread in the groove, resulting in faulty stitches.

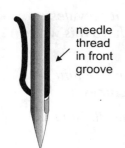

Size: Needle size refers to the shaft diameter. There are two sizing systems for needles. The European size refers to the needle size in hundredths of millimeters, ranging from 60 to 120. The American designation is an arbitrary number from 8 to 21. Often, manufacturers list both the European and American numbers, such as 70/10 — the number before the slash is the European size, and the number after the slash is the American size. Not all needle types come in every size. With both sizing systems, the larger the number, the larger the needle.

The sizing system of machine needles is opposite from the one used for handsewing needles. With machine needles, larger numbers mean larger needles. Handsewing needles always get smaller as their number increases, but the numbers are not consistent from one category to another.

You may also notice the numbers **130/705** on packages of needles. These are not a size code; rather, they refer to a "system" that has been standardized for sewing machines made since the early 60's. If your machine is older, check your machine manual or consult with your dealer.

Another code, the letter "**H**", appears on some packages of needles. It stands for "Hohlkehle" ("long scarf" in German). Long scarf needles are superior for sewing a zigzag stitch because the needle can get closer to the shuttle and bobbin.

Why have different sizes of needles at all? As a rule, finer fabrics require smaller needles and heavier fabrics require larger needles. In most cases, the heavier the fabric, the heavier the needle and the thread. For best results, use the finest needle small enough to pierce the fabric without leaving a hole, but large enough that the needle doesn't bend or break in the fabric during normal sewing. If you can't decide between two sizes of needles, use the smaller size. If skipped stitches present a problem, try the next larger size needle.

As with all aspects of sewing, *testing* with the project materials you intend to use is the only way to be sure of perfect stitching, especially when working with unfamiliar fabrics and threads.

Although it's hard to tell by looking, needles *do* get dull, and probably faster than you think. Even the slightest imperfection can damage fabric. If you're having problems with stitch quality or seam smoothness, your needle is probably getting dull or damaged. Synthetic fibers, including rayons and microfibers, dull needles more quickly than natural fibers. Needles often dull after only one or two garments, but don't try to sharpen needles by sewing on sandpaper!

Needles also develop *burrs* — sharp hook-like distortions of the point. They're caused by running the machine too fast or pulling or pushing the fabric too hard, and can also occur when the needle point hits something as you sew. Burrs can ruin your fabric and cause expensive damage to your machine. To test for a burr, slide the needle point in and out of a piece of nylon panty hose. If the needle catches on the hose, it has a burr, and you should discard it. You should also replace a bent needle.

The best needle is a new needle, so indulge yourself when starting a project and begin with a fresh needle. If you start having sewing problems, try a new needle. If the problem goes away, throw out the old needle — you won't want to use it again.

Cheap needles are usually a false bargain. They're weak, they break and bend easily, they cause skipped stitches, and they can damage your machine.

TIP: A patch of white on the presser foot shank helps with threading because it provides a contrasting background so you can better see the eye. If your machine does not have this white patch, you can "paint" one using white correction fluid.

TIP: Don't be afraid to try a more expensive European needle, no matter what machine you have. They can make your machine perform like one of the most expensive machines made.

TIP: For easy threading, slide the thread down the groove on the front of the needle, and it will go right through the eye.

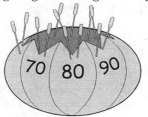

TIP: Store slightly-used needles in a pincushion you have labeled with a Sharpie marker.

TIP: To clean the bobbin area of your machine, use a bent pipe cleaner. Also use a cotton swab dotted with a small drop of your sewing machine oil.

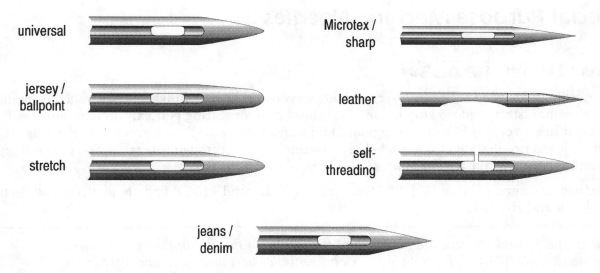

Basic Sewing Machine Needles

Universal

This needle is called universal because it sews most fabrics well. Several companies manufacture them, but Schmetz is one of the most widely available. You will use it most often, so it's fortunate that it's the least expensive choice. It works well on virtually all woven fabrics and the point is slightly rounded so it won't damage most knits. Universal needles have a long-scarf and have the "H" code somewhere on their package. They come in sizes 60/8, 65/9, 70/10, 75/11, 80/12, 90/14, 100/16, 110/18, 120/19, and in handy multi-sized packs. Size 80/12 is the most common needle used, so you should have plenty on hand.

NOTE: Schmetz makes *Round Shank* needles for older sewing machines and sergers. Ask your dealer to recommend the correct needle system for your older machine.

Singer Red Band

Use the red band needles for woven fabrics. These needles are made for Singer and Kenmore machines. Don't use them on European machines.

⚜ *TIP*: *Make a test sample with the exact thread, fabrics, interfacings, stabilizers, and battings that you are using in a project. It may be tempting to use up older threads, partially filled bobbins, and scrap fabric, but you won't know what results you'll get in your finished project.*

⚜ *TIP*: *Stock up! Keep a variety of needles in your sewing room so that you can experiment before beginning a project. Having the needles you need helps keep you going when you are sewing late into the night and your dealer isn't open.*

⚜ *TIP*: *Write the needle size on a small Post-It™ and stick it to your machine so you know what size needle is in the machine.*

⚜ *TIP*: *Use a 70/10 needle when sewing on Ultrasuede Light and an 80/12 needle for sewing on Ultrasuede.*

⚜ *TIP*: *You can use an extra-large 120/19 needle in place of a wing needle to create decorative holes in fine fabrics.*

Special Purpose Machine Needles

Jeans / Denim

This needle is designed for sewing very densely woven and heavily finished fabrics such as denim, corduroy, upholstery, and rip stop nylon. It is the choice for getting perfectly straight stitches because it has a very stiff shaft, sharp point, and slender eye. It will, however, cause great damage to knits. Jeans needles are also a good choice for topstitching through several layers, plus sewing and embroidering heavy weight fabrics.

These needles come in sizes 70/10, 80/12, 90/14, 100/16, and 110/18 and are identified by their blue shank and **H-J** code.

TIP: The 70 and 80 sizes are newer than the larger H-J needles and ideal for sewing Ultrasuede. The 70/10 J is a good choice for buttonholes on tapestry or uneven fabrics.

*TIP: If you are sewing on a microfiber and are out of **Microfiber / Sharp** needles, try using a 70/10 J jeans needle.*

TIP: If you run out of special quilting needles, use a 70/10 J for precise straight stitching.

Jeans Twin / Denim Twin

This heavy duty twin is made especially for denim and tightly woven fabric. Use it for uniform rows of topstitching on heavy fabrics. See page 12 for more information on twin needles.

This needle comes in twin-needle size 4.0/100 and is coded **H-J ZWI**.

Jersey / Ballpoint

This needle has a fully rounded tip that slips between knitted fibers instead of piercing them. It prevents damage and skipped stitches when sewing knits. The shank of this needle is copper-colored. It comes in sizes 70/10, 80/12, 90/14, 100/16, and handy multi-sized packs. Use this needle with polyester thread.

Jersey / Ballpoint needles are available in two point styles:

H-SES has a fine ball point for sewing fine knitted fabrics.

H-SUK has a medium ball point for sewing heavier knitted fabrics, elastics, and Lycra.

TIP: Do not use a ball point needle on silk. The fibers are too close together and too delicate, so the tip would tear the fabric.

Stretch

This needle has a slightly more rounded point than a universal needle. The eye is small and high up on the shaft, restricting the thread and protecting it from too much movement and friction. There is a tiny hump between the eye and the scarf that allows the thread to make a large loop on one side of the needle. This loop makes it easy to complete a stitch.

This needle, which is blue, is a good choice for sewing silk jersey, lingerie fabrics, synthetic leathers, synthetic suedes, and dense knits such as Lycra. They come in sizes 75/11 and 90/14 and are coded **H-S**. Use polyester thread with the stretch needles.

NOTE: Test stitch with both the ballpoint and the stretch needle. If there is no difference in stitch quality, use the stretch needle.

NOTE: If you have had problems with holes developing along the seamline of a knit garment after washing, the culprit was either a needle that was too large or a tip that was too round for the fabric.

TIP: Reduce sewing speed to prevent wavy or stretched seams. On lightweight knits, a narrow zigzag of 0.5 SW and a medium stitch length work better than the "knit stitch" programmed in many sewing machines.

TIP: Use a 90/14 for sewing on faux fur.

TIP: The stretch needle is a good needle for eliminating skipped stitches on older machines.

Stretch Twin

The stretch twin needles have special points to reduce skipped stitches on knits. These needles are great for hems and imitating fine ready-to-wear knits. See page 12 for more information on twin needles.

These needles come in sizes 2.5/75 and 4.0/75 and handy multi-sized packs. They are coded **H-S ZWI**.

Leather

The point is wedge-shaped for piercing the skins of real leathers and real suedes. Do not use these needles on faux leathers, faux suedes or fabric!

These needles come in sizes 70/10, 80/12, 90/14, 100/16, and 110/18 and are coded **H-LL**, **H-R**, or **NTW**.

Either a 70/10 or 80/12 **H-LL** needle is a good choice for sewing lightweight leathers such as deerskin or chamois.

TIP: Use the thinnest needle possible when sewing on leather. Use polyester thread and a stitch length of 9 - 11 stitches per inch. For topstitching leather, use 8 - 10 stitches per inch.

TIP: For sewing on faux leathers, use a 65/9 or 75/11 Universal needle and a polyester thread.

TIP: For sewing on patent leather, use a fine needle (70/10) and a stitch length of 3 mm.

TIP: For sewing on Ultrasuede light use a 65/9, 70/10, or a 75/11 Ballpoint needle. Use one of those needles, an 80/12, or a 90/14 for topstitching.

TIP: For sewing on Ultrasuede use a 75/11 or 90/14 stretch needle. For topstitching on Ultrasuede use a stretch needle or a 100/16 universal needle.

Quilting

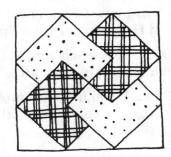

These needles have a thin, tapered deep point for sewing multiple layers. This design results in very little fabric damage when seaming and cross-seaming. Use them for machine piecing and machine quilting.

These needles come in an assorted size pack with three 75/11 needles and two 90/14 needles. The Schmetz brand has a green band at the base of the shank for easy identification. They are coded **H-Q**.

NOTE: Sewing through batting dulls a needle quickly, so change the needle often.

Self-Threading

These specialty needles are designed with a small slit at one side of the eye, making threading easy. Because of the slit, they are slightly weaker than regular sewing machine needles, so slow down your sewing speed and do not hold the fabric too taut.

These needles come in sizes 80/12 and 90/14.

Serger

Sergers manufacturers have not yet standardized needle systems, so consult your manual or dealer to select the correct needle. A needle that is even ¼" too long can seriously damage the loopers and other serger parts.

The Schmetz overlock needles have sharp points and are suitable for all fabrics. Two assorted packages are available:

- **BLX1** includes two 75/11s and three 90/14s.
- **DCX1** includes two 75/11s and three 90/14s.

Microtex / Sharp

These needles have a thin shaft and slim, sharp point for smooth seams with little or no damage to lightweight and delicate woven fabrics such as microfibers, batiste, sandwashed fabrics, and silkies. You may need several needles to complete a garment. Microtex / Sharp needles are a must for heirloom sewing.

The Schmetz brand is called Microtex / Sharp. These needles come in sizes 60/8, 70/10, 80/12, and 90/14. They have a violet band at the base of the shank for easy identification, and are coded **H-M**.

The Lammertz brand comes in sizes 70/10, 80/12, 90/14, and 100/16 and handy multi-packs.

✒ TIP: If you're having trouble getting even edge stitching or topstitching, try this needle.

✒ TIP: Use a 60/8 or 70/10 needle to prevent puckers when sewing seams in lightweight fabrics.

Singer Yellow Band

Use the yellow band needles to sew tightly knitted fabrics, to stitch with decorative threads, and to reduce or eliminate skipped stitches. Like the red band needles, these needles are made for Singer and Kenmore machines, so don't use them on European machines.

Spring

Schmetz manufactures these needles with an attached spring. They are designed for darning, free-motion embroidery, and free-motion quilting. The spring reduces fabric bounce in free-motion quilting and embroidery work. This needle may eliminate the need for a darning foot. Spring needles usually come with a universal size 80/12 needle.

Spring needles are now available in Jeans/Denim, Sharp, Quilting, and Embroidery.

🪡 *TIP: You should only need to buy one spring needle because you can replace the needle by carefully removing it from the spring. You can replace the spring needle with a 90/14 embroidery needle if you are very careful.*

🪡 *TIP: Don't forget to lower the presser foot bar when using this needle.*

🪡 *TIP: You may have to skip the final thread guide when using this needle.*

Teflon® Coated

Teflon® coated needles are designed for smooth, non-stick sewing on densely woven fabrics. Pentapco manufactures Teflon® coated needles in sizes 75/11, 90/14, and 110/16.

Topstitch

This extra-sharp needle is not as rounded as the universal point. The eye is twice as long and the front groove is deeper than the 90/14 universal needle. The position and the size of the eye help heavy topstitching threads form good quality stitches with polyester thread in the bobbin. Use this needle with its long eye to accommodate heavy thread without piercing large holes in the fabric. You can use the topstitch needle with some of the lighter weight decorative threads and metallic threads, as well as with two strands of regular sewing thread. The long eye makes it a bit fragile, causing it to break when sewing very heavy fabrics.

These needles come in sizes 70/10, 80/12, and 90/14, and are coded **N**.

NOTE: Topstitching is a single row or multiple rows of accent stitching. It can enhance or emphasize the garment edge or seamline. Topstitching has practical uses also, such as holding hems in place, stabilizing collars, lapels, and garment edges.

🪡 *TIP: Use a longer stitch length: 8 – 10 stitches per inch; 3 – 4mm stitch length. Don't make the stitches too long, as shorter stitches look straighter. Again, as with other stitching, sew a test sample first.*

🪡 *TIP: Sew slowly and with an even speed.*

Decorative Machine Needles

Hemstitch / Wing

This needle has two metal "wings", one on each side of the needle shaft, to help separate the fibers in woven fabrics to create a desired hole called hemstitching. Use this needle with a variety of decorative stitches to create heirloom stitching, such as the *point du prie* and *entredeux* stitches. For the best results, use crisp cotton fabrics, as blends do not retain the hole formed when stitching. Use the hemstitch / wing needle with care, as the flanges can damage fine fabrics and laces.

This needle comes in sizes 100/16 and 120/19.

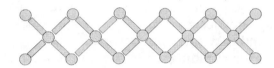

Example of a decorative stitch with a wing needle

Embroidery / Metallic

These needles are designed for trouble-free sewing with the new machine embroidery and decorative threads that have a tendency to break, split, or shred easily. The eye is large enough to accommodate heavy decorative threads, and the front groove is deep to reduce skipped stitches. It also has a very light ballpoint but not quite as round as a ballpoint needle. These needles are slightly thinner than size 90/14 universal needles. Embroidery needles are made to withstand the higher temperatures produced by decorative threads. These modifications help reduce skipped stitches, damaged fabric, and frayed thread.

Also use this needle when stitching both knit and woven fabrics.

- Use the 75/11 needles for 50/3 and 60/2 weight cotton, 40 weight rayon, Sliver, and Tinsel Lamé.

- Use the 80/12 needles for 30/2, 40/3, and 50/3 weight cotton, 40 weight rayon, metallic, Sliver, Tinsel Lamé, and two strands of thread through one needle.

- Use the 90/14 for 30/2 weight cotton, cordonnet, 30 weight rayon, metallic, Sliver, and two strands of thread through one needle.

NOTE: Free-motion embroidery or quilting puts a lot of strain on the needle, so use a good needle and change it often.

- ### *Schmetz Embroidery*

  Coded **H-E**, the Schmetz brand of embroidery needle is the Stick-Nadel Embroidery needle. It has a red band at the base of the shank for easy identification. It comes in an assorted size pack with three 75/11 needles and two 90/14 needles.

- ### *Metallica*

  Use these 80/12 Schmetz needles, coded **H-MET**, with metallic and flat-filament type decorative threads. The eye is double sized, the front groove is deep, and the scarf is longer. The size 80/12 is kinder to fabrics than the 90/14 stretch needle and the 90/14 embroidery needle.

- *Lammertz Metafil / Madeira Metallic*

   Coded **H-M**, this 80/12 embroidery needle is made from a specially treated alloy that withstands the higher temperatures generated by synthetic and metallic threads. It has a long eye with a friction-reducing coating, resulting in reduced thread stripping. The fine needle size is kinder to fabrics than the 90/14 stretch needle that was traditionally used for sewing with metallic threads. Replace the needle when the coating wears off after heavy use.

Twin / Double

Twin needles are coded **H ZWI, H-S ZWI, H-J ZWI, H-E ZWI,** and **ZWIHO**. They can only be used on front threading zigzag machines. Two needles are attached to a cross bar that has a single shank.

Twin needles have functional and decorative uses, including top stitching, decorative stitching, pin tucks, trapunto, hemming, and designer details. These needles are great for imitating better ready-to-wear, and they save time sewing hems. Using the **ZWI** needles ensures even rows of top stitching while creating attractive designer details.

Twin needles form a stitch with two parallel rows of straight stitching on the right side of the fabric. The bobbin thread forms a row of zigzag stitching on the wrong side of the fabric. If a pin tuck foot is used with a double needle, the bobbin thread draws the stitches up to form a small ridge or "tuck" in the fabric. Reduce needle tension if you want the stitches to lie flat and not form a pin tuck ridge.

The needle packages have two numbers to designate the needle size. The first number indicates the distance between the needles in millimeters, and the second number indicates the size of the needles. For example, a 2.0/80 needle has two 80/12 size needles that are 2.0 millimeters apart.

Twin needles are available in different sizes ranging from 70 to 100 and widths ranging from 1.6 to 8.0. Schmetz has a twin needle multi-pack that includes 1.6/70, 2.0/80, and 3.0/90 needles. See the *Twin Needles* chart on page 57 for more information on the twin needle sizes and uses.

See also Stretch Twins, Jeans Twins, Embroidery Twins, and Double Hemstitch for more information.

Threading Your Machine with a Twin Needle

Use two spools of thread. Place the spools on the spool holders as shown in the diagram. The left thread will feed off the back of the spool, and the right thread will feed off of the front of the spool.

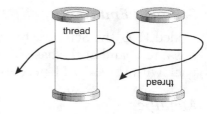

Continue threading your machine. Thread the left spool of thread on the left side of the tension disk and through the left needle. Then thread the right spool of thread on the right side of tension disk and through the right needle. Some machines sew better when both threads are on the same side of the tension disk. Sometimes, better results are achieved if one or both needle threads are *not* threaded through the last thread guide before the needle.

Checking the Stitch Width

When using zigzag or decorative stitch, select the twin needle setting on your machine or check the stitch width by turning the hand wheel manually through the entire stitch pattern. Make sure neither needle hits the presser foot. Even though some computerized machines have a double needle setting, it is important to check stitch width by manually turning the hand wheel. Machines are often preset for a specific double needle width. It is also possible that manually checking the stitch width through the entire stitch will allow the machine to complete the stitch, but when actually sewing, the needle will break. Pay particular attention to the needle when hand checking; the needle may bend slightly when manually stitching, but the speed of the machine sewing will cause the needle to break.

NOTE: Extra-wide twin needles require a specific minimum zigzag stitch width. The 6.0 needle requires a minimum 6.5mm zigzag, and the 8.0 needle requires a 9mm zigzag.

Double Hemstitch

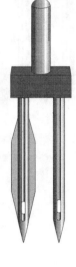

(**ZWIHO**) This needle has a wing needle on the left and a universal needle on the right to create a desired hole called hemstitching. Use it with a variety of decorative stitches to create heirloom stitching. Double hemstitch needles can only be used on zigzag machines that thread from front to back. As with the twin / double needles, be careful to check stitch width or select the sewing machine double needle button.

Jeans Twin

(**H-J ZWI**) See page 6 for more information on jeans twins.

Stretch Twin

(**H-S ZWI**) See page 7 for more information on stretch twins.

Embroidery Twin

(**H-E ZWI**) This twin needle has two embroidery needles attached to the single shank. See page 11 for more information on embroidery needles.

This needle comes in two different sizes 2.0/75 and 3.0/75.

Double Metallica Needle

This twin needle has two metallica needles attached to the single shank. See page 11 for more information on metallica needles.

This needle comes in size 2.5/80.

Extra Wide Twin

This needle comes in two different sizes 6.0/100 and 8.0/100. The 6.0 size can only be used on machines with a 6.5mm or greater stitch width, and the 8.0 size requires a 9mm minimum stitch width.

Drilling / Triple

Triple needles are similar to twin needles, but have three needles instead of two. Use triple needles for multiple rows of decorative stitches or to make two pin tucks at once. When using a triple needle, be careful of the stitch width, just as in using a twin needle.

These needles come in sizes 2.5 and 3.0 and are coded **H-DRI**.

*Example of a straight stitch
with a triple needle*

Hand Sewing Needles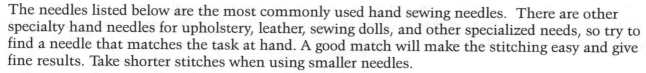

The needles listed below are the most commonly used hand sewing needles. There are other specialty hand needles for upholstery, leather, sewing dolls, and other specialized needs, so try to find a needle that matches the task at hand. A good match will make the stitching easy and give fine results. Take shorter stitches when using smaller needles.

Unlike machine needles, hand needle sizes are "backwards" — higher numbers mean smaller diameters and shorter lengths.

When stitching with large fibers, choose a needle with an eye large enough to accommodate the fiber. The needle should be large enough around to pierce the fabric and make an opening so the fiber can pass through the fabric without stressing the fiber or the fabric.

Basting

This needle is curved to make basting and tying quilts quick and easy.

Beading

These needles are very long and fine with a small eye. Use them for beading and couching down heavy fibers. They range in size from 10 to 15.

Calyx-Eyes / Self-Threading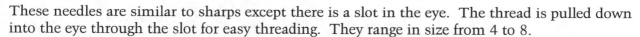

These needles are similar to sharps except there is a slot in the eye. The thread is pulled down into the eye through the slot for easy threading. They range in size from 4 to 8.

Chenille / Silk Ribbon

These needles are used for silk ribbon embroidery because of their large eyes and sharp points. You can also use this needle for sewing heavy fibers. Chenille needles range in size from 18 to 24.

Crewel

These needles have a sharp point with a long, narrow eye. They are good for stitching with embroidery floss, silk ribbon, and heavier fibers. They range in size from 1 to 10.

Darning

These large needles have a large eye. Smaller darners are good for those who have difficulty threading sharps and other hand sewing needles. Wool darners are good for working with heavy fibers, wide ribbons, and wool darning yarns. The cotton darning range in size from 1 to 9, and the wool darning range in size from 14 to 18.

Majestic 88

These are English needles with a special coating which permits easy stitching through cotton battings or difficult-to-needle fabric. Under normal use, the plating won't wear away or tarnish. This needle from Hapco comes in Betweens sizes 9, 10, and 12.

Milliners / Straw

These are long, narrow needles with a small, round eye. Because the needles are uniform in diameter, they are good for sewing beads onto fabric and stitching French knots. They're also used for *Baltimore Appliqué*, and range in size from 3 to 9.

Quilting / Betweens

These are short, fine needles with a short round eye. Use them for quilting and fine handsewing. They are also available with larger eyes, but this style may be hard to find. They range in size from 3 to 12.

Sharps

These fine, medium length needles with a round eye are the most commonly used hand sewing needles. Also use them for fine embroidery and hand sewing. They range in size from 5 to 12.

Tapestry

These stout needles have a long eye and a blunt point. Use them for pulled and drawn work and silk ribbon embroidery. They are also a good needle for drawing couching and bobbinwork fibers to the wrong side of the fabric. They range in size from 13 to 28.

What is Thread?

Webster's New World Dictionary defines *thread* as "a light, fine, stringlike length of two or more fibers or strands of spun cotton, silk, etc. twisted together and used in sewing."

Often, spools of thread will give the weight of the thread as a pair of numbers, such as **50/3**. The first number describes the weight or thickness of the thread. The **larger** this number, the **finer** the thread. The number after the slash is the number of plies or strands that are twisted together to form the thread.

Many of the better-quality threads are *cross-wound* on the spool. On a straight-wound spool, the threads appear parallel, but on a cross-wound spool, they almost appear "woven" or interlaced as shown at left. This winding technique ensures smooth thread flow off the spool and reduces stress on the thread, giving consistently superior stitch quality.

If possible, select thread on spools with smooth edges. Milled or notched edges can catch the thread and cause it to ravel, fray, or break.

Threads vary greatly in quality, and there are several things you should avoid. Some threads are fuzzy or flaky, and some have slubs (thick lumpy sections) or short fibers poking off the main strand. These threads are of poor quality and will break easily. Threads with "pokies" will leave the shorter fibers behind in your tension disks and bobbin area, potentially causing machine problems. Threads with uneven thickness or knots do not feed through the tension disks smoothly and result in poor quality stitches and weak seams. Long staple thread, the preferred choice, is strong and has a nice luster.

Generally:

- Delicate fabrics need smaller stitch lengths.

- Thicker threads need longer stitch lengths *and* looser machine tension settings.

Most spools give their lengths in meters. If you use yards, you can use this chart to convert from one to the other:

30 m =	33 yd	250 m =	274 yd	650 m =	711 yd
60 m =	66 yd	300 m =	328 yd	800 m =	875 yd
100 m =	109 yd	350 m =	383 yd	1000 m =	1094 yd
150 m =	164 yd	450 m =	492 yd	1100 m =	1204 yd
200 m =	219 yd	500 m =	547 yd	1675 m =	1833 yd

TIP: Some machines (even within a particular brand or model) seem to sew better with a particular brand of thread. Getting to know how your machine sews with the different brands of thread will help you determine the thread selection that is best for your machine.

TIP: If you have trouble finding a thread color that matches your fabric, try matching the value *rather than the shade. Often, a neutral gray of just the right value will blend in perfectly with a variety of dark, pale, or bright colors having the same value. Generally, choose thread a shade darker than the fabric as it will appear a bit lighter when stitched.*

TIP: For even bobbin tension, always wind onto an empty bobbin.

Basic Sewing Threads

Polyester Universal Sew-All

Polyester thread does not shrink or fade. The preferred polyester thread to use is long staple polyester. It is of superior quality, has a greater luster, is pliable, soft, and strong, and is very tolerant of sewing machine settings. Avoid polyester threads that stretch when pulled.

You can use polyester thread on almost any fabric, including silks. Dense or thick fabrics require the strength of polyester thread, as do seams in high-stress areas or places that might be abraded. Because it is stronger than cotton fabric, the cotton fabric might tear before the polyester thread breaks. Avoid using polyester thread on 100% cotton fabrics or for quilting.

High speed causes polyester thread to stretch as it is winding on a bobbin. The thread doesn't have a chance to relax until it forms a stitch. When it does relax, the thread contracts, causing puckered seams which you can't press out. Therefore, when winding bobbins, set your machine on the lowest speed setting or slow down the speed manually.

NOTE: Either cotton or polyester thread gives good results when sewing on silk. Experiment to see which thread is better for each project.

TIP: For sewing on knits, use a medium stitch length and reduce sewing speed to prevent wavy or stretched seams. For sewing on lightweight knits, use a narrow zigzag of 0.5 stitch width and a medium stitch length. This zigzag stitch is preferred over the knit stitch because the knit stitch puts too much thread in the seam.

- ### *Mettler Metrosene Thread*

  Mettler thread comes in a wide variety of colors and is an excellent quality long staple thread for nearly all sewing purposes.

- ### *Gütermann "All Purpose"*

  Gütermann thread comes in a wide variety of colors and is an excellent quality long staple thread.

Mercerized Cotton

Cotton is the most versatile fiber made into thread. Mercerizing, a chemical treatment, is sometimes applied to cotton threads to increase their luster and improve their strength. Cotton thread is excellent for sewing cotton and silk, and for quilting. The thread of choice is made from three plies of long staple cotton.

Cotton threads come in several different weights or thicknesses. For garment sewing, use 50/3 weight thread. For information on 30 and 60 weight threads, see pages 32 - 33.

Cotton thread does lose its strength with time, becoming brittle, so do not keep an extensive stash.

NOTE: Enhance the look of appliqué, buttonhole, satin, and decorative stitches by using cotton thread, which fills in the spaces between stitches. Cotton threads lay better on the fabric when stitched because they are softer and more flexible. They make beautiful rolled hems on both the sewing machine and serger.

TIP: If you sew with both polyester and cotton threads, store the polyester and cotton wound bobbins in two separate bobbin boxes so you can match the prewound bobbins to the same thread type. If possible, store the matching spool and bobbin together.

• **Mettler "Silk Finish"**

   This is a good quality long staple cotton thread. It comes in a wide range of colors, and the spools have purple printing for easy identification.

• **Gütermann "Natural Cotton Thread"**

   This 100% cotton thread is cross-wound on the spool, and is available in 100, 250, and 400 meter lengths.

Special Purpose Threads

Heirloom sewing / Fine Handsewing / Lingerie / Bobbin Threads

These threads were developed for fine handsewing, heirloom sewing, and for use in the bobbin when stitching with decorative threads for machine quilting, appliqué, embroidery, and decorative stitches. They are a fine thread, usually from 60 to 70 weight. Because they are so fine, they do not bunch up under the fabric, jam the machine, or distort fabric or stitches. Bobbin thread should be close to the weight of the needle thread. These threads are usually available only in white and black.

- *YLI Lingerie & Bobbin Thread*

  YLI Lingerie & Bobbin thread is a nylon thread with a special twist that creates a little stretch as you sew.

- *Sew-Bob*

  This lightweight, continuous filament nylon thread looks delicate but is very strong. It is available on 1000-yd and 1500-yd spools.

- *Madeira Bobbinfil*

  This thread is a super-fine 70 weight polyester thread.

- *Sulky® Bobbin Thread*

  This thread is a super-fine 70 weight polyester thread and is available on Sulky's exclusive snap spools.

- *J & P Coats Dual Duty Plus® Extra Fine*

  This cotton-covered polyester thread is a good solution for older sewing machines that have trouble sewing with the new fine-weight threads.

TIP: The bobbin systems of older machines are not calibrated for the finer weight lingerie threads. If you have an older machine and are experiencing difficulty with these threads, use regular polyester thread in the bobbin.

TIP: Be sure to wind bobbin threads slowly, as they will stretch with high speed winding, resulting in puckered seams.

Gimpe

This is a heavy cord-type thread that comes in black and white. Use it for corded pin tucks, corded buttonholes, and in easy machine gathering techniques.

Fishing Line

Fishing line (from the sporting goods department!) is used to add body or firmness to a rolled edge such as a ruffle. Lighter weight line gives a curly or wavy edge, and heavier line gives a firm, flared edge. Most often, a satin stitch or rolled edge stitch is used over fishing line.

Elastic Thread

Elastic threads consist of a blend of polyester or nylon and rubber. The most frequent use is in the bobbin for gathering, shirring, and decorative gathering effects.

Monofilament Thread

This translucent thread comes in fine and medium weights. The new nylons are soft to the touch and high in strength. They will not melt under an iron. Use a monofilament when you want an invisible thread. Professionals recommend this thread for invisible machine quilting. Use monofilament thread in sewing machines and sergers. They come in clear, for use on lighter colored fabrics, and smoke, for use on darker colored fabrics.

❉ *TIP: Monofilament thread has a lot of thread drag when sewing. Loosen the needle tension to counteract stitch difficulties.*

❉ *TIP: When filling plastic bobbins, fill only half full. Totally filled plastic bobbins tend to warp.*

- **YLI Wonder Invisible Thread**

  This is the thinnest monofilament available. *Quilter's Resource* recommends using this thread in both bobbin and needle for an invisible blind hem.

- **Sulky® Monofilament**

  This fine .004 weight polyester thread comes in clear and smoke on Sulky's® exclusive snap spools.

- **Coats Monofilament**

  This thread comes in clear and smoke on cardboard tube spools.

❉ *TIP: An empty Sulky, Gütermann, or Metrosene spool fits inside the large cardboard monofilament spool, making it feed off the spool smoothly.*

Fusible Thread: ThreadFuse™

ThreadFuse™ is a polyester thread twisted with a fusible nylon filament. The fusible fiber melts and adheres to whatever is pressed against it, leaving the polyester thread intact. It works on nearly all fabrics that can be ironed with steam. Its best use is in the bobbin or in either looper of the serger. When used in the lower looper, it serves the purpose of hemming appliqués and trims. You may need some tension adjustments to achieve a balanced stitch.

Use a zigzag stitch when possible to have more ThreadFuse™ exposed for secure fusing.

Always press with steam from the top side of the stitching, use a press cloth, and **never** allow the iron to touch the ThreadFuse™. Test first on a scrap of the same fabric you are using. Allow the fabric to cool before moving the fabric.

This thread is most often used for basting. You can separate fused fabric by pulling hard.

For basting, press for 12 seconds. For a more secure bond, increase fusing time.

This thread is also helpful for matching plaids, applying lace, inserting zippers, placing trims, applying appliqués, and in constructing bound buttonholes. It is useful for tacking down facings, hems, seams, seams on ravelly fabrics, patch pockets, bias tape binding, and wherever you want a thin line of fusible.

Water Soluble Basting Thread: YLI Wash-A-Way

These threads make removing both hand and machine basting stitches fast and easy. It is strong enough to hold a garment together for fitting. Use only on fabrics that can be washed.

Polyester Topstitching / Buttonhole Thread

Topstitching thread is a tightly twisted, heavy thread requiring a topstitching size needle or size 90 embroidery needle. Polyester and cotton wrapped polyester topstitching 30 weight thread is useful for decorative topstitching. Also use this thread for handworked buttonholes, cording buttonholes, making corded pin tucks, finishing edges, bobbin work, sashiko, and in easy machine gathering techniques. Use topstitching thread in the needle and an all-purpose polyester thread in the bobbin. Select a stitch length with about 8 stitches to the inch.

TIP: If you have trouble with this thread, try polyester thread in needle and topstitching thread in the bobbin or topstitching thread in both the needle and bobbin.

TIP: Because this thread is heavy, 55 yards or less are on a spool. Take yardage into consideration when purchasing threads for a project.

NOTE: For topstitching:

- Use a shade lighter than the garment fabric for a dressy, elegant effect;

- Use a shade darker than the garment fabric for a sporty look; or

- Use a color that contrasts with the garment fabric for a casual look.

- **Cordonnet**

    This polyester thread from Mettler is 30/3 and has 55 yards per spool. The spools have blue writing for easy identification.

- **Gütermann Twist**

    This polyester thread from Gütermann is 30/3 and has 33 yards per spool.

TIP: If you have problems with skipped stitches when topstitching, try using Sewer's Aid on the needle thread.

TIP: Make sure you start topstitching with a full spool and a full bobbin.

Hand Quilting Threads

Hand quilting threads have a glacé coating (a traditional wax coating applied to the surface of the thread) to keep them free of kinks and knots. Do *not* use this thread in the sewing machine because the coating will come off on the tension disks and other machine parts.

🪡 *TIP: Hand quilting thread is great for hand basting because it doesn't twist or knot.*

- *Mettler Hand Quilting Thread*

  This is an extra-strong, cotton-wrapped polyester thread with a waxed finish. This thread comes in 30 colors.

- *Gütermann Hand Quilting Thread*

  This 100% cotton thread has a special glacé finish. It comes in 50 colors.

Machine Quilting Threads

- *Mettler Silk Finish 100% Cotton Machine Quilting Thread*

  This thread is suitable for both machine and hand quilting. It is 40/3, comes in 30 colors, and the spools have brown writing for easy identification.

- *DMC Quilting Thread*

  DMC's quilting thread is 30% cotton and 70% polyester, and can be used for both hand and machine quilting. This thread is strengthened with a unique InterGlazed™ process, a treatment interwoven into the fibers. It is available in 30 colors.

- *Gütermann Natural Cotton*

  This 100% mercerized cotton thread is available on 100 and 250 meter spools.

Silk Thread

Silk thread sews well on silks and woolens. It is smoother, more elastic, and stronger than cotton thread yet very fine. Another advantage of silk thread is that it remains lustrous and strong over time. Silk thread is ideal for basting and hand quilting, and can also be used for hand sewing, machine sewing, decorative detailing, machine embroidery, needle art, heirloom sewing, and heirloom serging. It can be hard to find and is naturally a bit more expensive. Choose colorfast silk thread.

TIP: Silk thread is great for hand or machine basting because it leaves no hole when you remove the stitches.

- **Gütermann Silk Thread**

  This thread comes on 100m spools and is available in 196 colors.

- **Silk Buttonhole Twist**

  This thread can be hard to find, but it's worth the effort. Its wonderful subtle sheen gives a hand-stitched look to machine crazy quilt stitches.

- **Tire Silk Thread**

  This 50/3 thread is made from the highest grade of silk reeled directly from quality silk cocoons. It comes in 70 colors. Elly Sienkiewicz recommends this thread for Baltimore Album quilts.

- **YLI 1000 Denier Silk Sewing Thread**

  This 100-weight silk sewing thread can be hard to find. It comes on 200-meter spools in 48 colors. It is used for sewing, embroidery, appliqué, and making bamboo rugs.

- **YLI Kanagawa Silk Sewing Thread**

  This 50/3 thread is also made from the highest grade of silk reeled directly from quality cocoons. Use it for heirloom sewing, machine embroidery, basting, and garment construction.

- **YLI Kanagawa Silk Stitch**

  This heavy 30/3 silk thread is ideal for topstitching, machine quilting, crazy patch machine embroidery stitches, and serging. Use it in the needle and loopers of a serger.

TIP: Silk thread is usually the best choice for sewing on wool because it makes the seams almost invisible.

Blue Jean Thread

Topstitch jeans with the same thread used in the industry.   Use a size 90/14 Jeans needle with this thread.

- ### *Signature Blue Jean Thread*

  This heavy-duty, dull gold thread comes on 75-yard spools. It is a cotton-wrapped thread with a polyester core.

- ### *YLI Jeans Stitch*

  This 100% polyester 30 weight thread comes in 22 colors in addition to blue jean gold.

Upholstery Thread

Upholstery thread is useful in both hand and machine sewing where high seam strength and durability are required. Use it on most types of leather, vinyl-coated fabrics, denim, canvas, upholstery, and carpet materials.

NOTE: On most heavy materials, use at least a size 16/100 needle and 8 – 10 stitches per inch.

- ### *Gütermann Upholstery Thread*

  This polyester thread comes on mini cones in twelve colors.

Woolly Nylon

- ### *YLI Woolly Nylon*

  This is an untwisted, texturized and crimped nylon thread that fluffs out when stitched, making it a popular thread for practical and decorative use. It has considerable stretch, good recovery, and fills in nicely for decorative edges. Because it stretches, it is ideal for sewing all types of knits. When used in the serger, it makes a nice rolled edge. It makes comfortable seams and prevents raveling because the fiber tightens up after serging. It comes in a wide variety of solid and gradated colors.

  Woolly Nylon comes in three varieties:

  - Original Woolly Nylon
  - Woolly Nylon Extra (three times heavier than original Woolly Nylon; used only in serger loopers)
  - Metallic Woolly Nylon (single strand of metallic filament twisted with the nylon)

☛ *TIP: Use a press cloth and low temperature setting when pressing Woolly Nylon, as it will melt.*

☛ *TIP: For rolled hems, if you can't adjust the tension in the lower looper tight enough to roll the hem, use woolly nylon in that looper.*

Serger Thread

Serger thread is a short staple cotton, two-ply thread and is slightly finer than all-purpose polyester thread. Since several threads create a serged seam, thinner serger threads reduce bulk. Serger thread has a special finish applied to it to make it extra smooth for high speed serging. Serger thread is not recommended for use in a regular sewing machine, as two-ply, short staple cotton produces weak seams. Two brands of serger threads are *Maxi-Lock* and *Metrosene*.

TIP: For decorative looks, use virtually any of the decorative threads in serger loopers. Consult your serger manual, the Singer Sewing Reference Library *books, and the* Palmer Pletsch Creative Serging *books for more information on successful serging with decorative threads.*

Decorative Threads

Decorative threads include embroidery cotton, rayon, and metallic. Cotton threads create smooth, clear embroidery with a flat look, rayon threads create a smooth lustrous look, and metallic threads reflect light and create a shinier look.

Try to find decorative threads on cross-wound spools, which provide a smoother thread flow. Notch-free, smooth-edged spools help prevent the thread from becoming damaged.

Decorative threads are ideal for adding designer details, appliqué, buttonholes, charted needlework, cross stitch, cutwork, decorative serging, decorative stitches, embroidery, freehand machine embroidery, French hand sewing, hand work, heirloom sewing, lace-making, mock hand work, monogramming, needlelace, needleweaving, pin tucks, punch needle, quilting, rolled edges, rolled hems, shadow work, topstitching, and thread sketching.

NOTE: Loosen the needle tension or thread the bobbin thread through the bobbin finger (only on some machines). This will pull the needle thread slightly to the wrong side of the fabric, eliminating the little dots of bobbin thread that show on the right side of the fabric.

NOTE: Use bobbin thread in the bobbin when using decorative threads. White bobbin thread is fine, unless you are using a dark fabric.

NOTE: The rule for using decorative threads is *experiment, experiment, experiment* to see what works best on your machine with your thread and your fabrics. Always stitch a test sample after changing needles, threads, or tension settings.

RULES FOR USING DECORATIVE THREADS

- Sew slowly.

- Use an embroidery needle. (refer to *Decorative Needle & Threads Chart*, page 56)

- Change your needle more frequently when using decorative threads because they create a lot of friction, which is hard on the needle.

- Reduce needle thread tension. To loosen needle tension, move tension dial to a lower number on some machines; move to the minus range on other machines.

- Use fine bobbin thread in the bobbin and wind this thread very slowly.

- Clean & oil machine frequently, following the directions in your machine manual. Even a little piece of metallic thread in the bobbin area can cause sewing problems.

- Use a stabilizer when doing decorative stitches. You can add more than one piece of stabilizer if you experience problems.

- Match the presser foot to the stitching and threads. See *Machine Accessory Feet*, page 43.

- Keep an eye on the rayon and metallic spools as you sew. They may jerk during sewing and spin backwards a little, causing the thread to wrap around the spool pin. If this happens too often, try using a foam spool ring such as The Finishing Touch Spool Ring or a thread stand such as *The Thread Pro* and the *Thread Palette*.

- If you have trouble with fraying and breaking thread, use *Sewer's Aid* on the spool of thread. *Sewer's Aid* is a silicone lubricant that reduces friction and heat build-up. It's colorless and absorbs into the thread. Don't use it on the mylar threads, because the thread does not absorb it. Try *Lub-A-Thread* to apply liquid silicone to the thread before going through the needle's eye. Also try using a stand alone thread stand such as *The Thread Pro* or multiple machine spindles such as *Thread Palette*.

- It's okay to start collecting a thread stash. Having a lot of wonderful fibers around spurs creativity and can be very therapeutic.

TIP: There is no need to have decorative threads in both the needle and bobbin unless both sides of the fabric will show.

TIP: Use a lightweight static cling vinyl strip such as the Thread Wrap or Thread Saver to keep decorative threads from unwinding in storage. These are also helpful for guiding threads onto machine. Loosely wrap the strip around the spool while sewing.

TIP: Using variegated thread can sometimes result in a "blocky" look. To prevent this, use two variegated threads together in a single needle.

TIP: Add depth to a color by combining it with a dark colored thread. Give life to a dull thread color by adding a lighter color or metallic thread.

TIP: If you have followed all of the rules and suggestions above and still have problems, try turning the thread upside down or placing it in an Old-Fashioned size glass set on the table behind the machine.

TIP: Any time you change a decorative stitch or setting, sew up a test sample first.

TIP: We recommend hand washing or dry cleaning to care for embellished work.

TIP: We recommend creating a stitch sample notebook using a 3 ring binder. It's easy and fun to make your own reference book. Cut pieces of pale fabric 15" X 10" and fold in half so you have a piece 7½" X 10". Sew row after row of different stitches using different colors and thread choices. Store these pages in plastic page protectors in your binder and you have a wonderful reference guide. You don't have to have a fancy computerized machine to create a wonderful decorative stitches book - use decorative threads and sew up samples of all of your utility stitches in addition to any decorative stitches.

TIP: Use a press cloth and low temperature setting when pressing Woolly Nylon, as it will melt.

Tanne

Tanne is a 100% mercerized cotton embroidery thread. It is available in five weights: 80, 50, 30, 20, and 12.

Tanne 80/2 is the most widely available size and is the thinnest machine thread available. It lacks strength and breaks easily, so its use is limited to heirloom sewing and sewing on lace.

Embroidery Cotton

- ***30 weight Machine Embroidery Thread (many manufacturers)***

  This heavier cotton thread is ideal for embroidery and decorative sewing.

- **Mettler 30 Wt. Regular Machine Embroidery Thread**

  This 100% Egyptian cotton thread comes in solid and gradated colors. The spools have orange printing.

- **60 weight Machine Embroidery Thread (many manufacturers)**

  This cotton thread is one quarter the weight of normal sewing thread. It's ideal for French handsewing, embroidery, and decorative sewing. It's also a good choice for buttonholes on lighter weight fabrics, and is fine enough to use in the bobbin when using cotton or rayon threads in the needle. This thread is recommended for machine piecing and quilting miniature quilts.

- **Mettler Fine 60 Wt. Machine Embroidery Thread**

  Use this 100% Egyptian cotton thread for stained glass appliqué and Harriet Hargrave's invisible appliqué. The spools have green printing.

- **80 weight Machine Embroidery Thread (many manufacturers)**

  Use this fine weight cotton thread for heirloom sewing and embroidery work.

- **Madeira 30, 50, and 80 Wt. Cotona Thread**

  This 100% Egyptian cotton thread is double-mercerized. The 30 and 50 weight are two-ply and come in 36 colors. The 80 weight is one-ply and comes in 12 colors.

Rayon

Rayon thread is a high luster thread most often used for machine embroidery and other embellishment on sewing machines, embroidery machines, and sergers. It comes in a wide variety of weights and textures. Rayon threads are thin and slippery, so you may have to adjust machine tensions for successful sewing. They are springy and may jump out of the tension disks or slip down and wind on the spool pin. If you experience difficulty, use a thread stand.

Rayon thread is **not** for piecing or sewing seams. It loses strength with age or when wet.

The rayon threads listed below are machine washable in cold water, using a delicate cycle. Do not use chlorine bleach or optical brighteners (non-chlorine bleaches such as Clorox 2). Press from the wrong side on a soft towel using a low temperature setting. You may also dry clean these threads.

Avoid off-brand rayon threads, as their performance and quality are often poor.

TIP: Wind bobbins at a medium speed. To avoid loose and tangled bobbin threads when winding a bobbin with rayon, lightly pinch thread with your finger between the last thread guide and the bobbin.

TIP: Buttonholes look great when stitched in rayon thread. For best results, use an 80/12 HJ needle.

- **40 weight (many manufacturers)**

  This rayon thread is ideal for machine embroidery, embroidery machines, and decorative stitches. It is the most readily available rayon thread size.

- **30 weight (many manufacturers)**

  This heavier rayon thread is ideal for machine embroidery, embroidery machines, and decorative stitches. It's 33% thicker than 40 weight thread, so it fills in between the stitches better.

- **Sulky® Rayons**

    Sulky® rayon threads, available in solid, variegated, and gradated shades, come in 102 colors in 30 weight and 193 colors in 40 weight. Sulky® rayons are cross-wound on the spool, and both ends of the spool snap open for easy release of the thread. Color numbers and size are conveniently printed on each spool for easy identification. Some Sulky® rayons come on economical large size spools.

- **Madeira Rayons**

    Madeira 40 weight rayon threads come in a wide variety of solid and variegated colors. Some of the more popular colors also come on large size spools.

- **Madeira Neon Thread**

    These threads are available in fluorescent and light reflective colors. They are great for sports and safety wear, children's clothing, and work clothes.

- **Finishing Touch™**

    These 30 weight rayon threads come in a wide variety of solid and variegated colors and have been specially treated so that the thread will not "skin" or draw up when washed. The color number is conveniently printed on the end of the cardboard spool.

- **Coats Mez Alcazar**

    These 40 weight rayon threads are available in a wide variety of colors and are usually found at Pfaff sewing machine dealers.

- **Mega-Sheen™**

    These rayon threads are relatively new on the market, and may be hard to find. Check with an Elna dealer. They are 30 weight and come in a wide variety of solid and variegated colors on 1094-yard cones.

- **Natesh**

    This is a fine rayon thread, nearly a 50 weight. It may be hard to find. Use it for machine embroidery.

Metallic

Metallic threads are available in a wide variety of types, weights, and combinations of fibers. They reflect light for added dimension and sparkle. Most metallic yarns are a combination of fine metallic yarn, rayon, polyester, and metal. Use them for machine embroidery and other embellishments on sewing machines, embroidery machines, and sergers.

Choose metallic threads based on fabric and finished appearance. Avoid metallics which tend to fray badly or have a lot of the core fiber showing, and don't use metallics that feel heavy or stiff in the machine needle.

If you experience difficulty with metallic threads, there are two silicone products available: *Sewer's Aid* and *Sew Slick*. These products reduce friction and static electricity and help eliminate skipped stitches and breakage. Use **sparingly** on thread spool. If you still have trouble, you may also use them sparingly on bobbin thread, needle eye, and presser foot. Owners of older machines who try everything and still have problems should wind the metallic on the bobbin, loosen top tension, use polyester thread in the needle, and sew with the wrong side of the fabric up.

The metallic threads listed below are machine washable in cold water on the delicate cycle. As with rayons, avoid chlorine bleach and optical brighteners. Press from the wrong side on a soft towel, using a low temperature setting. You may also dry clean these threads.

- **Sulky® Metallic**

    Sulky Metallic is ideal for machine embellishment. This thread comes in 36 solid, gradated, and variegated colors and on Sulky's® snap spools. Some Sulky® metallics come on economical large spools.

- **Madeira Dazzle Metallic**

    Use Dazzle Metallic for machine embellishment. It comes in a variety of solid, gradated, and variegated colors.

- **Madeira Supertwist**

    This thread blends two fibers to produce a special texture or sparkle effect. It comes in forty-two basic colors and fifteen opalescent colors on 1100-yard spools.

- **Madeira FS Jewel**

    This thread is a blend of rayon and metallic fibers. Each color is twisted with a black fiber that gives the thread depth and texture. More than twenty colors are available on 612 yard spools.

- **YLI 601 Fine Metallic**

    YLI Fine Metallic thread is one of the thinnest metallic threads available. This thread is available in single or multiple strands on 500-yard cones and smaller spools. They are a good choice for embroidery machines and sergers.

- **Mettler Metallic**

    These metallic threads are a bit hard to find and come in very few colors. The color number is conveniently printed on the spools.

Mylar

Mylar (or tinsel thread) is a flat, highly reflective, ribbon-like, polyester thread. Embroidery designs take on a stunning luster when sewn with this flat thread. It was designed for fewer breaks and is strengthened so it does not fray. Because it's flat, it does not completely fill in satin stitches or embroidery motifs that contain satin stitch elements. It sews open decorative stitches well. You can dry clean, machine wash and dry these threads. Dry and press at a low heat setting.

For best results, place the spools in a vertical position.

- **Sliver**

    Sulky® Sliver is metallized with aluminum to make it brilliantly reflective. It's available in 24 colors on the Sulky® snap spools.

- *Stream Lamé Tinsel Thread*

  Tinsel lamé is available in a wide variety of colors. Two of the colors are spun with aluminum, giving them the ability to change color when the light shifts.

- *Prizm™ Hologram Thread (also known as Madeira Jewel)*

  Tiny pinpoint holograms are laid in a continuous, random fashion on a micro-thin polyester film. This highly reflective, light catching thread comes in six colors and is machine washable and colorfast.

Acrylic

- *Madeira Burmilana*

  Use a size 90/14 needle when embroidering with this woolly thread. It comes in 115 colors, and is also great for decorative serging.

- *Renaissance Thread*

  This wool / acrylic blend resembles wool yarn. Use it in the sewing machine with a 110/18 needle. It is machine washable, machine dryable, and drycleanable. Also use for serging, hand embroidery, bobbin work, machine embroidery, and cross stitch.

- *YLI UltraSheen*

  These acrylic threads are available in a wide variety of solid and variegated colors on plastic cones.

Decorative Threads for Couching & Bobbinwork

Use these heavier threads for couching, passementerie, decorative serging, pin weaving, weaving, knitting, punch embroidery, handwork, duplicate stitch, machine bobbin embroidery, embellishment, needlepoint, weaving, making fringe, braids, trims, doll hair, and jewelry.

TIP: Serge slowly when using decorative threads.

TIP: Serger stitch length should be 2 – 3 when using decorative threads.

TIP: The thicker the thread, the looser the serger tensions.

About Couching

Couching is an easy technique for using threads, fibers, and trims that are too large to go through the needle eye. Simply machine stitch over the thicker threads and trims to anchor them to the base fabric. A presser foot grooved on the underside glides easily over heavier fibers while guiding them in place. Suitable presser feet include appliqué, braiding, cording, couching, embroidery, open-toe, piping, and ribbon feet. Match the thickness of the couching fibers to the depth of the foot groove. You may want to use a couching foot with a braiding guide to hold the yarn straight in front of the presser foot. Use a zigzag or decorative stitch just wide enough to cross over the fibers without piercing them. If the bobbin thread should show on the right side of the base fabric after loosening the needle thread tension, use a polyester thread that matches the base fabric in the bobbin.

heavier thread

needle thread

TIP: Use the Hands free Multi-Thread Minder to keep several different couching threads under control and tangle-free.

About Bobbinwork

Bobbinwork (also called cabling, reverse couching, or reverse embroidery) is an easy technique for creating a lot of texture and depth by using fibers that are too large to go through the needle eye. Use these fibers in the bobbin and sew from the wrong side of the fabric. This technique is also ideal for adding detail and sewing curves and angles not possible to do when couching the fibers from the right side of the fabric. You can use ribbon floss, perle cotton, chenille yarns, crochet thread, "goldfingering" yarns, Candlelight, and Glamour.

Begin by hand-winding the fiber on the bobbin or use a slow bobbin winding speed while pinching the fiber to provide the tension and serve as a thread guide. Do not fill the bobbin completely. Loosen the bobbin tension, consulting your machine manual. It is helpful to have a second bobbin case so you do not have to repeatedly change the tension on the bobbin used for regular sewing. Some machines may require you to by-pass the bobbin tension altogether.

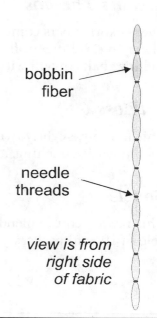

bobbin fiber

needle threads

view is from right side of fabric

Before you adjust the screw in the bobbin case, use a Sharpie marker to mark the screw's original position so you can reset it for normal sewing. Turn the screw slowly over a white terry cloth towel or piece of flannel. If the tiny screw comes out, it won't bounce out of sight.

Although you may have to tighten the needle tension, begin with regular tension. Test stitch. When the tensions are correct, the bobbin fibers lay flat on the right side while the stitches on the wrong side will look neat.

Use polyester sewing thread, rayon, or metallic decorative thread in the needle. Suitable presser feet include braiding, cording, couching, embroidery, piping, and ribbon feet. Match the thickness of the couching fibers to the foot groove.

To prepare the fabric for stitching, place the fabric on table wrong side up. Slide outer ring of embroidery hoop under fabric. Place inner ring on top of fabric. Centering design fabric in hoop, tighten fabric in hoop so that it is "drumskin" tight.

Stitch from the wrong side of the fabric. To begin, hold the thread tails securely and take a couple of stitches. Leave the needle down in the fabric. Pull the thread tails to draw the bobbin fiber up to the wrong side of the fabric to prevent tangles. Keep the thread tails out of the way of the stitching. When finished, use a tapestry needle to pull bobbin fibers to the wrong side and tie off tails. Because some fibers and threads are slippery, secure knotted ends with a seam sealant like Aleen's Stop Fraying or Fray Check™.

TIP: Use either the same color thread in the needle and bobbin or use contrasting colors. Monofilament thread in the needle gives a nice look, also.

TIP: You can do bobbinwork with straight stitch, free-motion, and decorative stitches built into your sewing machine. Experiment with all of the possibilities to see what you and your machine can create.

NOTE: In addition to the fibers listed here, try specialty fibers found in needlepoint, knitting, and cross stitch shops. These handwork fibers are luscious, come in very small quantities, and are much more expensive than any of the decorative threads listed here.

Accents Threads

These exotic fibers come in 15 yard packages of a single color. They are washable and dryable. There are 28 different fibers available in a variety of textures, such as chenille, rayon, polyester, and fuzz balls (nylon with dots). Use these fibers for wearable art, doll hair and pin weaving.

ArtFloss 6

This four ply, slightly twisted rayon thread is soft and super-shiny. Use it for serging, top stitching, bobbin work, couching, sashiko quilting, hand embroidery, knitting, crochet, and cross stitch.

Bouclé

This rayon / cotton blend is variegated and has a nubby texture. Sixteen different colors are available in 10 yard packs.

Chenille

This 100% rayon fiber comes in 43 solid and variegated colors, and is sold in 10 yard packs. It has a tufted, velvet-like pile.

YLI Candlelight Metallic Yarn

This soft, lightweight, metallic thread is available in 20 colors.

Madeira Decor

Use this medium weight, untwisted, soft, satiny, high luster, 100% rayon thread for serging, bobbinwork, and embroidery machines. It's more fragile than twisted threads, and is available in 40 colors.

YLI Designer 6

Use this rayon filament thread for serging, bobbinwork, and embroidery machines. It's similar to Madeira Decor, and comes in 30 colors.

Designer Threads

This multi-thread pack has five different color-coordinated fibers on one card. There are 30 different packs available.

Frappé

This cotton / rayon blend is a soft nubby fiber that comes in solid and variegated colors. Four solid and variegated muted shades are sold in 10 yard packs.

Madeira Glamour Metallic Yarn

This is a soft metallic thread available in many colors. It's 65% viscose rayon and 35% metallic polyester, and is available in 25 colors. It is similar to YLI Candlelight.

Metallic Ribbon Floss

These fibers, which come in eight colors, have all of the advantages of rayon Ribbon Floss with extra sparkle. This is also a delicate fiber and can't tolerate a lot of wear.

On The Surface

This multi-thread card comes with five yards each of six coordinated colors. These fibers are a wonderful complement to the *Cherrywood* hand-dyed fabrics. A fiber manipulation lesson is included on the back of the card. Twenty-two different cards are available.

Pearl Crown Rayon

This 100% rayon thread has a tight twist and a soft sheen. It comes in 44 colors.

Pearl Cotton

This all-cotton thread has a loose twist and a soft sheen. It comes in a variety of weights and colors.

Radiance

This rayon / lurex blend is a soft, metallic, "frize-type" fiber that comes in solid and variegated colors. Eighteen different colors are available in 10 yard packs.

Rayon Ribbon Floss

This fiber is a 100% rayon mini ribbon which is braided rather than woven, resulting in a stitch that fills out nicely. This soft fiber, which is available in 30 colors, can resemble the look of silk fibers in some applications. It's a delicate fiber and can't tolerate a lot of wear.

Ribbon Thread

This ribbon is similar to Ribbon Floss, but is harder to find.

100% Pure Silk Ribbon

Silk ribbon is very soft and supple; it slides through fabric effortlessly. This ribbon is popular for use in silk ribbon embroidery. Silk ribbon comes in several different widths: $1/16$" (2mm), $1/8$" (4mm), $1/4$" (7mm), $1/2$" (13mm), and $1\frac{1}{4}$" (32 mm).

Elegance Ribbon Collection™ Hand-dyed Silk Ribbon

This 4mm silk ribbon has been hand-dyed with 3 – 4 colors shaded into it.

Heirloom Sylk Synthetic Silk Ribbon

This ribbon is soft and supple, just like the 100% silk. It is an economical alternative for use in silk ribbon embroidery, and comes in the same sizes as the 100% silk.

Special FX

This is a variegated chenille fiber available in 15 different colors, 15 yards to a pack.

Machine Accessory Feet

This is not an exhaustive list of machine accessory feet, but the ones listed here are particularly useful for embellishment. Check with your machine dealer to see if a particular foot is available for your machine. Generic feet will fit many machines. Little Foot, Ltd. and Creative Feet™ make special feet that fit nearly all machines.

Appliqué / Embroidery / Satin Stitch or Zigzag

This foot has a groove on the bottom to accommodate a heavy build-up of wide satin and decorative stitches. Some appliqué feet have "open toes" or are clear, giving a good view of the stitching path.

Darning Foot / Quilting Foot / *Big Foot*

Use this foot for free-motion quilting. The *Big Foot*, manufactured by Little Foot, Ltd., is a large foot which helps to hold fabric down against the bed of the machine while quilting.

Blind Hem

This foot has a fabric guide and a stitch bar that ensures the right stitch tension for "invisible" hemming. This foot, as well as the edgestitch foot, can be used for edgestitching and appliqué.

Braiding / Couching / Cording

This foot has either a one large hole and deep groove for couching one thick fiber or the foot has several holes or grooves for couching several fibers at once.

Cordonnet Foot

This foot has a small hole to hold a thin fiber in place for couching, gathering, or making corded pin tucks.

Gathering

This foot allows you to gather a single layer of fabric or gather one layer of fabric and stitch it to another layer of flat fabric in one step.

Little Foot™ / Patchwork / ¼" Foot

This foot helps you stitch an accurate ¼" seam. The *Little Foot*™ is manufactured by Little Foot, Ltd. and is also marked for stitching an accurate ⅛" seam.

Overcast / Overlock Foot

This foot has a fabric guide and bar that holds fabric and stitches flat, making it great for a satin stitch edge finish.

Pearls & Piping™

This foot is manufactured by Creative Feet™ and has a deep channel to pass smoothly over cording, decorative fibers, crosslocked beads, and rhinestones up to ¼" in thickness.

Pin Tuck

This foot has from three to nine grooves on the bottom. These grooves serve as guides for previous rows of pin tucking. See more about stitching pin tucks on pages 12 - 13 and on the *Twin Needle Chart*, page 57.

Satin Edge™

This foot is manufactured by Creative Feet™ and has an adjustable guide and open toe for appliqué, topstitching, and edge stitching.

Sequins & Ribbon Foot™

This foot from Creative Feet™ has an adjustable guide that holds sequins, ribbons, elastic, and braids flat for easy couching. Additional guides are also available for different widths of ribbons, etc.

Straight Stitch / Jeans

This foot is for sewing straight seams only. It is good for sewing thick, hard fabrics and sewing over thick seams. It helps give straight, even stitches on slippery fabrics.

Tailor Tack / Fringe ..

This foot has a vertical bar down the center of the foot. Zigzag stitches form over this bar, creating loops. This foot is great for creating dimensional stitching and short fringe.

Teflon®

The Teflon® coating on the bottom of this foot is good for stitching over plastic, leather, and other difficult fabrics.

Other Helpful Products

Publications

- *The Creative Machine Newsletter, Open Chain Publishing*

  This 48-page quarterly forum is for people who love sewing machines and sergers the way others love cars or computers — questions and answers about machines; extensive book, video, and pattern reviews; articles, resource listings, information exchange, and lots of laughs.

- *OmniStitch News*

  A quarterly newsletter for embellishment enthusiasts. It gives information about new products, patterns, and techniques, specifically for OmniStitching and other embellishing.

- *Sew News*

  A monthly fashion sewing publication that deals with the latest in new sewing products, techniques, projects, and sewing machines. The focus is on sewing for you, your home, and your family.

- *Sewing Update*

  This bimonthly newsletter features fashion-sewing how-to's by professionals, plus innovative ideas, detailed sewing techniques, questions / answers, and information on new products and patterns.

- *Serger Update*

  This monthly newsletter features a wide variety of innovative serger how-to's from fashion to home dec, by top serger experts, plus the newest techniques, products, and tips.

- *Threads*

  A bimonthly, how-to magazine celebrating garment sewing and embellishment, needlearts, quilting, and related crafts. The magazine is reader-written and provides high quality, in-depth technical information. It's intended to teach and inspire; it's clear, engaging, and readily accessible.

Stabilizers

Stabilizers provide necessary backing and support. They eliminate shifting, puckering, and sliding of fabrics when doing appliqué, buttonholes, embroidery, free-motion work, punch needle, charted needlework, and monograms. They make it easy to move or turn the fabric without getting snagged on the feed dogs. Use stabilizers for temporary body and transferring designs. Most come in pre-cut packages or on bolts, and are available in different weights.

Depending on their type, stabilizers are usually removed after sewing by tearing them away, dissolving them in water, or disintegrating them with heat from an iron. Which one to use is up to you unless a project requires a particular type.

Tear-Away Stabilizers

Tear-away stabilizers are very helpful, but they tend to distort stitches somewhat when torn away, and they can leave "whiskers" or "eyelashes" behind. Because the stabilizer remains under the stitching, match the weight of the stabilizer to the weight of the fabric. Heavy and "crisp" stabilizers need to be cut away with scissors, not torn, or they will distort your stitches and fabric.

- *HTC Easy Stitch* ™

  Easy Stitch is a non-woven stabilizer that is evenly perforated with small holes for easy removal.

- *Sulky® Tear Easy, Stitch & Tear®, Tear Away Soft*

  These are lightweight stabilizers.

- *Tear Away Crisp*

  This stabilizer works well with heavier fabrics and monogramming on towels.

- *Stitch and Ditch*

  This thin paper stabilizer does not leave a residue of powder or dust in the machine and bobbin area. It has a low acid content, is easy to tear away, and does not dull the machine needle. It is also good for paper piecing, quilting, and heirloom sewing.

- *Filmoplast Stic, Firm Hold, Sulky® Sticky*

  These stabilizers adhere to your fabric without adhesives, leave no residue on fabric, and can be torn away from the stitches. They are designed for use with machine embroidery hoops and napped fabrics such as velvet, velveteen, and Ultrasuede®.

- *No Whiskers Tear Away*

  Clotilde's tear-away does not leave small fibers showing around the edges of the stitches when it is removed.

- *Reynolds Freezer Paper*

  This freezer paper from your kitchen cupboard is also good for use as a stabilizer and in freezer paper appliqué. Press the shiny side of the freezer paper to the wrong side of the fabric with a dry iron. The paper will dull needles quickly.

Iron-on Tear-Away Stabilizers

These stabilizers are more flexible than plain tear-aways, yet give the weight needed for embroidering on knits.

- **Sulky® Totally Stable**

    Totally Stable is an iron-on stabilizer that is easily torn away from stitching, leaving no sticky residue. It does not have to be ironed to the fabric to provide stability.

- **Jiffy Tear**

    This is an iron-on tear-away.

- **Press-N-Tear Soft** and **Press-N-Tear Crisp**

    These are temporary iron-on stabilizers that come in two weights.

Rinse-Away Stabilizers

Rinse-away stabilizers have the advantage of not adding extra layers to the fabric. They do not leave "whiskers" behind. They are more expensive than tear-away stabilizers.

NOTE: Use rinse-away stabilizers on fabrics and smaller projects that can be washed.

NOTE: Store the rinse-away stabilizers in a Zip-Loc® type of plastic bag. When exposed to air, they can dry out and become brittle, or they can absorb too much moisture from the air and be too moist to use on fabric.

TIP: *Use the rinse-away stabilizers when monogramming or embroidering terry cloth towels. Place the rinse-away on the right side of the towel, and use a tear-away underneath the fabric. The rinse-away will keep the stitches from being buried in the terry loops.*

TIP: *The rinse-away stabilizers are also great for stabilizing lightweight fabric when making rolled hems.*

TIP: *Tear away the excess stabilizer, then rinse to completely remove.*

TIP: *Use two layers of the rinse-away when you want a heavier stabilizer.*

- **Sulky® Solvy, Aqua-Solv™, HTC RinsAway™, YLI Solv-it, Melt Away™, Wash-A-Way, Madeira Avalon®**

    These stabilizers come in small packages or on the bolt. They're similar to each other and work well. Avalon comes packaged as a 9.8" strip, convenient for use in the sewing machine embroidery hoop.

- **GlissenGloss Melt-A-Way**

    This stabilizer is removed in hot water. The utensils used in removing this stabilizer can't be used in food preparation.

- **Perfect Sew**

    Perfect Sew is a liquid stabilizer that brushes on to fabric. It is removed by rinsing.

- *Sew Stable*

  This liquid stabilizer brushes on to fabric and is removed by rinsing.

- *Starch*

  Mix old-fashioned liquid starch with water and dip the fabric in the solution. When the fabric is dry, press, and stitch.

- *Sullivan's Spray Fabric Stiffener*

  This stabilizer comes in as liquid brush-on and aerosol spray. Both are removed by rinsing in water.

- *Light Fabric Stiffener*

  This spray is stiffer than spray starch and is removed by rinsing in water.

Iron-Away Stabilizers

These products are heat sensitive, disintegrate with a hot, dry iron, and then can be brushed away. They are often more expensive than the tear-aways. Be careful not to scorch your fabric while pressing, as they sometimes take a while under the iron to disintegrate.

NOTE: These products are called "vanishing muslin" in the UK and Australia.

- *Sulky® Heat Away™, Heat & Brush, Michelle Pullen's Vanish-a-Way®, Burn Away Stabilizer, Vanishing Muslin*

  Use these products to stabilize fabric that you wouldn't want to get wet or if you don't want to wait for it to dry.

- *Hot Stuff!!*

  This stabilizer is removed by short bursts of heat from the iron. It can even be removed by placing it in the sun.

Thread Aides

- ### *The Finishing Touch Spool Ring*

  This is a pack of two foam rings that you can place under thread spools to reduce static electricity. The rings also prevent the threads from puddling and getting caught under the spool.

- ### *Sewer's Aid*

  This is a nonstaining liquid silicone. Use on metallic threads to control breakage.

- ### *Lub-A-Thread*

  This applicator attaches to your machine and applies liquid silicone to the thread *after* it has gone through thread guides. Use on metallic threads to control breakage.

- ### *Thread Pro*

  This stand gives you the option of using a horizontal or vertical thread position. It also has a piece of foam under one of the thread guides to control breakage. The foam can be treated with a silicone lubricant. This stand is also great for those machines that have difficulty stitching with monofilament thread.

- ### *Thread Palette*

  This plastic disk holds up to four spools of thread and fits on the spool holder of machines and sergers. It is a great tool for blending threads when sewing, couching, and serging.

- ### *"Hands Free" Multi Thread Minder*

  This plastic guide, which sticks to your machine with suction cups, guides up to five couching fibers in front of the needle / presser foot. It is a great tool for blending threads when sewing and couching.

- ### *Thread Wrap and Thread Saver*

  These lightweight static cling vinyl strips keep decorative threads from unwinding, getting dirty, and tangling during storage. You can also use them to provide additional tension on the thread when threading the machine by wrapping the vinyl strip very loosely around the spool while sewing.

- ### *E-Z Winder*

  This kit comes with spools and an E-Z Winder that you attach to your bobbin winder spindle. Make one or more additional spools of thread from one cone of serger or woolly nylon thread. Also wind decorative threads or yarn on spools to be used on your serger or sewing machine.

Great Resources

If you can't find the supplies mentioned in this book at your local sewing machine dealer, quilt shop, specialty fabric shop, smocking shop, or heirloom sewing shop, check these great resources.

Clotilde, free notions catalog, *800-772-2891*

The Creative Machine Newsletter, Open Chain Publishing, *PO Box 2634, Menlo Park, CA 94026-2634*

In Cahoots, free pattern catalog, *800-95-CAHOOTS or* **http://www.in-cahoots.com**

Majestic 88 needles, check with local quilt shop or call **Hapco** at *314-698-2102*

Nancy's Notions, free notions catalog, *800-833-0690*

SCS, free catalog, *800-542-4727*

Sew-Art International, free catalog, *800-231-2787*

SpeedStitch, free catalog, *800-874-4115*

Summa Design, free brochure, *513-454-0943*

Threadline, free brochure, *800-237-4354*

Thread Pro, check with local Viking dealer or call Pamela Burke at *214-369-1614*

Thread Shed, free catalog, *704-692-5128*

TreadleArt, catalog $ 3 (refundable with order), *310-534-5122*

Web of Thread, free catalog, *502-575-9700*

Suggested Further Readings

Periodicals

Creative Bernina Magazine, available at Bernina dealers

The Creative Machine Newsletter, Open Chain Publishing, *415-366-4440*

OmniStitch News, *142 Braewick Rd, Salt Lake City, UT 84103*

Pfaff Club Magazine, available at Pfaff dealers

Serger Update, *PO Box 1790, Peoria, IL 61656*

Sewing Update, *PO Box 1790, Peoria, IL 61656*

Sew News Magazine, *PO Box 3134, Harlan, IA 51537-3134*

Threads Magazine, *800-283-7252*

Books

10, 20, 30 Minutes to Sew by Nancy Zieman and other books by author

Claire Shaeffer's Fabric Sewing Guide by Claire Shaeffer and other books by author

The Complete Book of Machine Embroidery by Robbie and Tony Fanning

Power Sewing by Sandra Betzina

More Power Sewing by Sandra Betzina

Mother Pletsch's Painless Sewing by Palmer & Pletsch

Singer Sewing Reference Library, Cy DeCosse Inc.

Heirloom Machine Quilting and *Mastering Machine Appliqué* by Harriet Hargrave

The Complete Book of Machine Embroidery and *The Complete Book of Machine Quilting, 2ⁿᵈ Edition* by Robbie and Tony Fanning

Creative Machine Art by Sharee Dawn Roberts

In Cahoots® Needles and Threads Chart

Fabric	Thread selection	Needle selection	Stitch length
Delicate: Chiffon Fine lace Gauze Organza Tulle Voile	Polyester Universal Sew-All Heirloom sewing thread Silk thread Fine machine embroidery thread 60 / 2	Universal 60 / 8 — 65 / 9	12 — 20 spi (1mm - 2mm)
Light: Batiste Crepe de chine Handkerchief linen Lamé Rip-stop nylon Sandwashed rayon Sandwashed silk Synthetic sheers	Polyester Universal Sew-All Fine machine embroidery thread 60 / 2 Mercerized Cotton 50 / 3 Silk thread	Universal 70 / 10 — 75 / 11 Microtex 60 / 8 — 70 / 10	12 — 18 spi (1.5mm - 2mm)
Microfiber	Polyester Universal Sew-All	Microtex 60 / 8 or Jeans 70 / 10	12 — 18 spi (1.5mm - 2mm)
Jersey interlock Silk jersey Single knits Tricot	Polyester Universal Sew-All Woolly nylon (in bobbin or serger loopers)	Universal or Jersey / Ballpoint or Stretch 70 / 10	12 — 18 spi (1.5mm - 2mm)
Medium Light: Challis Chambray Charmeuse Pongee Satin Wool crepe	Polyester Universal Sew-All	Universal 70 / 10 — 80 / 12	12 — 15 spi (1.5mm - 2mm)
Ultrasuede Light	Polyester Universal Sew-All	Jersey / Ballpoint 65 / 9 — 75 / 11 or Stretch 75 / 11 or Jeans 70 / 10	12 — 15 spi (1.5mm - 2mm)
Cotton knits Polar light Spandex Swimsuit fabric Wool jersey	Polyester Universal Sew-All Woolly nylon (in bobbin or serger loopers)	Universal or Jersey / Ballpoint or Stretch 70 / 10 — 80 / 12	12 — 15 spi (1.5mm - 2mm)
Lycra	Polyester Universal Sew-All	Jersey / Ballpoint H-SUK 70 / 10 — 80 / 12	12 — 15 spi (1.5mm - 2mm)
Medium: Broadcloth Chintz Corduroy Curtaining Faille Flannel Linen Silk linen Silk noil Taffeta Velveteen Wool flannel	Polyester Universal Sew-All Mercerized cotton 50 / 3	Universal 70 / 10 — 80 / 12 Jeans 80 / 12	10 — 15 spi (1.5mm - 3mm)

Fabric	Thread selection	Needle selection	Stitch length
Medium (continued):			
Microfiber	Polyester Universal Sew-All	Microtex 70/10 — 80/12 or Jeans 70/10 or Quilting 75/11	10 — 15 spi (1.5mm - 3mm)
Ultrasuede	Polyester Universal Sew-All	Stretch 75/11 — 90/14 or Jeans 80/12	10 — 15 spi (1.5mm - 3mm)
Bouclé jersey Double knit Sweatshirt fleece Velour	Polyester Universal Sew-All Woolly nylon (in bobbin or serger loopers)	Universal or Jersey / Ballpoint or Stretch 80/12	10 — 15 spi (1.5mm - 3mm)
Medium heavy:			
Bengaline Brocade Damask Drapery Felt Gabardine Quilted fabrics Tapestry Tweed Twill Velvet Vinyl	Polyester Universal Sew-All Cotton 40/3	Universal 80/12 — 90/14	10 — 12 spi (2mm - 3mm)
Denim	Polyester Universal Sew-All	Jeans 80/12 — 90/14	10 — 12 spi (2mm - 3mm)
Fake fur Swimsuit fabric Polarfleece	Polyester Universal Sew-All	Universal or Jersey / Ballpoint or Stretch 80/12 — 90/14	10 — 12 spi (2mm - 3mm)
Lycra Spandex	Polyester Universal Sew-All Woolly nylon (in bobbin or serger loopers)	Jersey / Ballpoint H-SUK 80/12 — 90/14	10 — 12 spi (2mm - 3mm)
Heavy:			
Canvas Drapery fabric Fur Heavy coating Sailcloth Upholstery Vinyl	Polyester Universal Sew-All Upholstery	Universal 90/14 — 110/18 or Jeans 90/14 — 100/16	8 — 10 spi (3mm)
Denim	Polyester Universal Sew-All	Jeans 90/14 — 100/16	8 — 10 spi (3mm)
Fake fur	Polyester Universal Sew-All	Universal or Jersey / Ballpoint or Stretch 90/14	8 — 10 spi (3mm)
Very Heavy:			
Canvas Duck Upholstery Work denim	Polyester Universal Sew-All Upholstery	Universal or Jeans 16/100 — 18/110	6 — 10 spi (3mm)

In Cahoots® Decorative Needles and Threads Chart

Thread Selection	Needle Selection	Bobbin Thread
30/2 Cotton Thread	Topstitching 90 / 14 or Embroidery 80 / 12 – 90 / 14 or Jeans 80 / 12 – 90 / 14	Fine bobbin thread
60/2 Cotton Thread	Universal 70 / 10 or Embroidery 75 / 11	Fine bobbin thread or 60/2 Cotton Thread
Cordonnet or Topstitching Thread	Topstitching 90 / 14 – 100 / 16 or Embroidery 90 / 14	Polyester
2 Strands of thread through one needle	Topstitching 80 / 12 – 90 / 14 or Embroidery 75 / 11 – 90 / 14	Fine bobbin thread
J. & P. Coats Dual Duty Plus ® Extra Fine	Microtex 70 / 10 or Jeans 70 / 10 – 80 / 12 or Quilting 75 / 11	Same
30 Wt. Rayon Thread	Embroidery 90 / 14	Fine bobbin thread or 60/2 Cotton Thread
40 Wt. Rayon Thread	Embroidery 75 / 11 – 80 / 12	Fine bobbin thread
Metallic Thread	Embroidery 80 / 12 – 90 / 14 or Metallic 80 / 12 or Metallica 80 / 12 or Topstitching 90 / 14	Fine bobbin thread or matching metallic
Mylar Threads	Universal 80 / 12 or Embroidery 75 / 11 – 90 / 14 or Metallic 80 / 12 or Metallica 80 / 12	Fine bobbin thread
Acrylic Thread	Topstitch 110 / 18 or Embroidery 90 / 14	Fine bobbin thread or polyester

ꙮIn Cahoots® Twin Needle Chart ꙮ

Remember to select double needle button (if available)
and manually check stitch width to ensure that needles do not hit foot

Size	Use	Machine foot
1.6 / 70 1.6 / 80	Pin tucking on delicate fabrics, decorative effects	9 groove pin tuck *or* appliqué
2.0 / 80	Pin tucking on delicate fabrics, decorative effects	7 groove pin tuck *or* appliqué
2.5 / 80	Pin tucking on delicate fabrics, decorative effects	7 groove pin tuck *or* appliqué
3.0 / 90	Pin tucking / Topstitching on light to medium-weight fabrics, decorative effects	5 groove pin tuck *or* appliqué
4.0 / 80 4.0 / 90 4.0 / 100	Topstitching on medium to heavy-weight fabrics, decorative effects	3 groove pin tuck *or* appliqué
6.0 / 100	Topstitching, decorative effects — straight stitch **use only on machines that have 6.5mm zigzag**	Appliqué *or* open toe appliqué
8.0 / 100	Topstitching, decorative effects — straight stitch **use only on machines that have 9mm zigzag**	Appliqué *or* open toe appliqué
4.0 / 100 *Jeans / Denim*	Topstitching on denim and dense fabrics	Appliqué *or* open toe appliqué
2.5 / 75 *Stretch*	Topstitching / hemming light to medium-weight knits	Appliqué *or* open toe appliqué
4.0 / 70 4.0 / 75 *Stretch*	Topstitching / hemming medium to heavy-weight knits	Appliqué *or* open toe appliqué
2.0 / 75 *Embroidery*	Decorative effects with decorative threads	7 groove pin tuck *or* appliqué
3.0 / 75 *Embroidery*	Decorative effects with decorative threads	5 groove pin tuck *or* appliqué
3.0 *Drilling / Triple*	Topstitching, decorative effects	Appliqué *or* open toe appliqué

Index

A

appliqué
    18, 20, 23, 24, 25, 31, 33, 37, 43, 44, 48

B

bobbin
    cleaning 4
    tension 2, 19, 23, 31, 37
    winding 19, 20, 23, 24, 31, 33, 37
bobbinfil 23
bobbinwork 18, 37, 38, 39
burr 4

C

cabling. *See* bobbinwork
catalogs 53
cotton. *See* fabric: cotton
couching 17, 18, 37, 38, 51
    crosslocked beads 44
    foot 43
cross-wound 19

E

embroidery
    silk ribbon 18
entredeux 11
eye 3

F

fabric
    cotton 11, 20
    cotton knit 2
    denim 6, 28
    knit 5, 6, 7, 9, 11, 20, 28, 49
    leather 7, 17, 28, 44
    lingerie 7
    Lycra 6, 7
    microfiber 4, 6, 8
    patent leather 7
    silk 6, 7, 8, 20
    suede 7
    synthetic leather 7
    Ultrasuede 5, 6, 7
    Ultrasuede light 5, 7
    upholstery 6, 17, 28
feet. *See* presser feet
foot. *See* presser feet
free-motion 38, 48
    embroidery 9, 11
    quilting 9, 11, 43
front groove 3

G

gathering 23, 24, 25, 43

H

hemming 7, 9, 12, 24, 25
    blind 43
    invisible 43
    knits 2
    rolled 20, 28, 31, 49

M

machine
    cleaning 4, 31
meters
    converting to yards 19
monogramming 31, 48, 49
    towels 48, 49

N

needle
    ballpoint 6
    basting 17
    beading 17
    betweens 18
    calyx-eyes 17
    chenille 17
    crewel 17
    darning 17
    denim 6
    denim twin 6
    double 12
    double hemstitch 13
    drilling 14
    dulling 4
    embroidery 11
        Metafil 12
        Metallica 11
        Schmetz embroidery 11
    embroidery twin 13
        double Metallica 13
    extra wide twin 14
    handsewing 3
    hemstitch 11
    jeans 6
    jeans twin 6, 13
    jersey 6
    leather 7
    Majestic 17
    microfiber / sharp 6
    Microtex / sharp 8

In Cahoots ®

Setting the new standard in wearable art patterns

Sheer Illusions

These eight embellishment techniques are sheer fun!

The soft hues of the *Sheer Illusions* palette create a pleasant flow of colors reminiscent of impressionist paintings and colorwash quilts. Instead of using many small blocks of fabrics for color blending, *Sheer Illusions* creates watercolor effects by combining layers of sheer fabrics. This pastel palette is a classic for every woman.

Detailed machine setup directions for each technique and tips on bobbin work are included.

Great Squares

Create your own fabrics, then combine them to make the multi-colored, multi-patterned, and multi-textured Great Squares vest.

This pattern has seven different embellishment techniques and a new way to piece squares. Learn exciting ways to make pin tucks and pleats. You'll love the incredibly detailed instructions and drawings.

Great Squares now includes a supplement for the embroidery machines and popular wool flannels, as well as valuable information about decorative threads and specialty needles. Detailed machine setup directions for each technique help beginners and experienced sewers.

Order now! Call 1-800-95-CAHOOTS (1-800-952-2466) or FAX 1-770-992-9678

Mosaic Magic

Mosaic Magic has a distinctive style with a flattering design.

Use this great adaptation of Seminole piecing to create your own colorful vest. If you are a quilter who has never sewn a garment before, this is a great first project. All you need are beginning sewing skills — most of the sewing is straight seams.

This pattern has incredibly thorough directions and helpful drawings. It includes directions for making quick and easy continuous bias binding.

Weaving is everywhere!

Learn In Cahoots' unique weaving techniques to create a striking one-of-a-kind garment – maximum style with minimum effort. Designed with a feminine style in mind, this vest is versatile and great for travel. The soft and supple weaving creates a blend of color and texture. The *Easy Woven Vest* is definitely a designer look — wearable art has never been so classy or so easy!

Pattern includes a SpeedWeaving™ needle and EasyWeave™ directions for better results in half the time! Incredibly thorough instructions and simple finishing methods help you make your fully-lined vest.

Easy Woven Vest now includes a supplement with helpful tips and several options for using trims and wider ribbons.

Easy Woven Vest

To help you be your creative best, all In Cahoots patterns include:

- 🐎 Classroom-tested techniques and instructions
- 🐎 Thorough machine set-up charts for each embellishment technique
- 🐎 Accurate, step-by-step instructions for each technique
- 🐎 Complete garment finishing instructions that teachers and students will love
- 🐎 Complete supply lists
- 🐎 Multi-sized from Small to Extra Extra Large

Order now! Call 1-800-95-CAHOOTS (1-800-952-2466) or FAX 1-770-992-9678

Moonstruck

The Moonstruck Vest is a magic play of color, light, and texture.

It's exciting to create your own fabrics and sew this flattering vest. Combine metallic threads, couching fibers, and specialty fabrics while learning five easy and fun embellishment techniques. Three of these techniques are In Cahoots' originals.

This pattern has incredibly thorough directions and clear drawings. Detailed machine set-up directions include needle and thread selections plus tension and stitch settings.

Great Beginnings is your blueprint for vest success!

Create your own one-of-a-kind vest with our most versatile pattern! Display your patchwork, fabric manipulation, and embellishment skills. In Cahoots' *Great Beginnings* vest pattern covers all the construction details and allows you to concentrate on creating your fabrics.

Terrific for teachers and intermediate to advanced sewers, it's the first pattern to provide you with incredibly thorough instructions, detailed drawings and supply list for:

- Four front design options combining five interchangeable pattern pieces
- Four finishing methods, including topstitching, reversible, bound, and piped
- Four back styles
- Two optional pocket designs

Great Beginnings

Your Blueprint for Vest Success!

Our customers are saying...

- "It's just like having the teacher in your sewing room!"
- "The designs are flattering... the length is perfect!"
- "Great directions!"
- "I ordered one of your patterns, and it was so easy to follow that I have to order the rest!"

Order now! Call 1-800-95-CAHOOTS (1-800-952-2466) or FAX 1-770-992-9678

The Guide to Success with Needles & Threads

An *In Cahoots*™ book
by Debbie Garbers and Janet F. O'Brien

If you sew, you need Point Well Taken*!*

This invaluable book includes information on basic needles & sewing threads. It also includes in-depth information on special-purpose needles and threads as well as complete information on decorative needles and threads. With its helpful drawings, it's easy to read, easy to follow, and easy to use.

- Includes information on couching and bobbinwork
- Thorough, helpful charts for Basic Needles & Threads, Decorative Needles & Threads, and Twin Needles
- Wonderful tips and hints to improve your sewing results

You'll want our needles & threads charts at your fingertips!

We've put years of experience and research onto two handy laminated charts! From our book *Point Well Taken*, the charts help you make smart decisions when selecting needles and threads.

- Our *Sewing Chart* covers all weights of fabric, from delicate (such as silk organza) to very heavy (such as canvas). It's a quick reference for matching fabric, thread, needle, and stitch length.
- Our *Decorative Chart* is a reference for matching needles, decorative threads, and bobbin threads. It also includes information on twin needles.

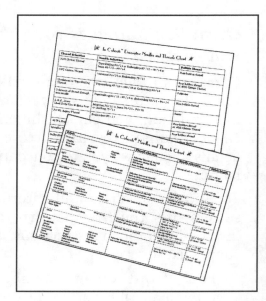

Our customers think Point Well Taken *is terrific!*

- "Absolutely fabulous!"
- "The tips are great!"
- "An excellent book... love the hints!"
- "There's nothing else out there like it!"

- "We're really impressed with the book!"
- "Can't wait to see what you do next!"
- "It's exceptional!"
- "This book will be around for a long time!"

Visit our full-color catalog and information center on the Internet:

http://www.in-cahoots.com

Order now! Call 1-800-95-CAHOOTS (1-800-952-2466) or FAX 1-770-992-9678

In Cahoots Order Form

PO Box 72336
Marietta, GA 30007-2336   •
770-641-0945   •
FAX 770-992-9678   •

800-95-CAHOOTS (orders only)
email: orders@in-cahoots.com
web: http://www.in-cahoots.com

Date: _____

Name: _____

Address: _____

_____

City: _____ State: _____ Zip: _____

Phone: _____ FAX: _____

Code	Quantity	Description	Price	Amount
1017	_____	Mosaic Magic Vest	$9.00	_____
1018	_____	Easy Woven Vest	$10.00	_____
1019	_____	Moonstruck	$10.00	_____
1020	_____	Great Squares Vest	$11.00	_____
1021	_____	Great Beginnings Vest	$12.00	_____
1022	_____	Sheer Illusions Vest	$12.00	_____
1101	_____	*Point Well Taken* Book	$12.90	_____
1201	_____	Sewing Chart	$4.00	_____
1202	_____	Decorative Chart	$4.00	_____
		Subtotal		_____
		Shipping / Handling		_____
		Total		_____

Shipping Charges

Each book $3.00
First pattern $2.50
Each additional pattern
.... add $0.50

Customer signature: _____

All prices in US $ — subject to change without notice
Orders sent outside US shipped prepaid plus postage

VISA and MasterCard orders call
1-800-95-CAHOOTS (1-800-952-2466)
In Georgia: 770-641-0945